# TABLE OF CONTENT

## Chapter 1: Early Life and Swim

- Childhood in Florida and discovery of swimming .......... 1
- Training and early competitions .......... 2
- Olympic dreams and setbacks .......... 4

## Chapter 2: Around the World .......... 8

- Embarking on a series of endurance swims .......... 8
- Crossing the English Channel and other iconic bodies of water .......... 10
- Exploring the world through swimming and advocacy .......... 12

## Chapter 3: The Impossible Dream .......... 14

- Contemplating the Cuba-Florida swim .......... 14
- Training for the extreme challenge .......... 16
- Facing criticism and skepticism .......... 19

## Chapter 4: The First Attempt (2011) .......... 21

- Attempting the swim with a team of 33 .......... 21
- Facing jellyfish stings and strong currents .......... 22
- Decision to end the attempt .......... 23

## Chapter 5: Recovery and Rededication .......... 26

- Reflecting on the failure and rebuilding strength .......... 26
- Training with a new team and strategy : .......... 27

## Chapter 6: The Second Attempt (2012) .................................................. 31
### Setting out again with a modified approach .................................... 31
### Overcoming jellyfish bites and exhaustion ...................................... 33
### Success after 53 hours of swimming ................................................ 35

## Chapter 7: Triumph and Legacy ............................................................. 38
### The historic accomplishment and its impact .................................. 38
### Inspiring others with her determination ........................................ 40
### Continued advocacy for ocean conservation .................................. 42

## Chapter 8: Beyond the Swim .................................................................. 44
### Writing, speaking, and sharing her story ........................................ 44
### Establishing a foundation for water sports and youth development .... 46
### Continuing to pursue challenges ...................................................... 48

## Chapter 9: Facing Challenges ................................................................. 51
### Overcoming setbacks and obstacles ................................................. 51
### Dealing with doubt, criticism, and injuries ..................................... 53
### The importance of perseverance and resilience ............................. 55

## Chapter 10: The Power of Belief ............................................................ 57
### The role of self-confidence and determination .............................. 57
### Visualizing success and overcoming fear ....................................... 58
### Inspiring others to achieve their own goals ................................... 60

## Chapter 11: The Transformative Journey ................................................. 63

*The transformative nature of endurance swimming* ....................... 63

*How swimming has shaped her life and perspective* ....................... 65

*The importance of finding meaning and purpose* ........................... 67

## Chapter 12: Training and Technique ................................................. 70

*Details of her training regimen and swimming technique* ............... 70

*The role of nutrition, hydration, and sleep* ....................................... 72

*Strategies for improving speed and endurance* ................................ 74

## Chapter 13: Teamwork and Support ................................................. 76

*The importance of a supportive team and crew* ............................... 76

*Collaborating with experts and scientists* ......................................... 78

*The role of camaraderie and motivation* ........................................... 79

## Chapter 14: The Cuba-Florida Swim: In Depth ................................ 83

*A detailed account of the planning, preparation, and execution of the swim* .................................................................................................... 83

*Facing unpredictable weather, wildlife, and physical limitations* ...... 85

*The emotional and mental challenges of the journey* ....................... 86

## Chapter 15: Environmental Advocacy ............................................... 89

*Nyad's passion for ocean conservation* ............................................. 89

*Raising awareness about marine pollution and ocean health* ........... 91

*Inspiring action through storytelling and activism* ..........................92

# Chapter 1: Early Life and Swimming Journey

## Childhood in Florida and discovery of swimming

Diana Nyad's story, as told in "The Pursuit of the Impossible," is deeply entwined with the turquoise waters of her native Florida. Born in 1949, she grew up in a world saturated by the ocean's influence. The rhythm of the tides, the whispering breeze, and the sun-drenched beaches became the soundtrack of her youth. This immersion in the natural world, particularly the vast expanse of the Atlantic Ocean, would profoundly shape her life and ultimately lead her to an extraordinary journey of athletic achievement.

The Florida of Nyad's childhood was a tapestry woven with the threads of both coastal serenity and the thrill of adventure. Her parents, both teachers, instilled in her a love for exploration and a sense of wonder about the world. The beach, a mere stone's throw from their home in the vibrant city of Miami, became her playground. This proximity to the ocean fostered an early and intimate connection with its power and mystery. . 

Her first foray into the water was not a planned event, but rather a serendipitous moment of discovery. The memory, as recounted in her book, resonates with the childlike curiosity and fearless spirit that would define her later years. One afternoon, during a family trip to Key West, a playful Nyad found herself perched on a lifeguard stand. As she gazed at the clear turquoise waters, a sudden urge to jump in took hold. With a mix of excitement and trepidation, she plunged into the unknown. This seemingly insignificant act marked the beginning of a lifelong love affair with the ocean, a love that would propel her to unimaginable heights.

The experience, simple as it may appear, was transformative. The cool embrace of the water, the gentle movement of the waves, the feeling of weightlessness - these sensations awakened a deep and instinctive connection with the ocean. This primal connection, woven into the fabric of her childhood, would continue to shape her life in ways she could not have imagined at the time. .

Florida's abundant coastline provided an endless playground for young Diana. She spent countless hours swimming, diving, and exploring the hidden coves and inlets of the Florida Keys. These early experiences fostered a sense of independence and an unyielding determination to push her limits. This exploration was not just about physical prowess; it was a journey of self-discovery, a quest to understand the boundless possibilities of her own potential. .

The Florida waters became her sanctuary, a place where she could escape the demands of everyday life and embrace the freedom of movement. The ocean's vastness mirrored the limitless possibilities of her dreams. It was within these waters that she began to develop her exceptional swimming abilities, honing her skills through countless hours of practice and an insatiable thirst for challenge. .

The impact of her Floridian upbringing is undeniable. The sun-kissed beaches, the turquoise waters, and the endless horizon of the ocean became the canvas upon which her life unfolded. It was here, in the heart of Florida, that the seed of her extraordinary athletic journey was planted. This early connection to the water, nurtured by the idyllic surroundings of her youth, would eventually blossom into a lifetime of adventure and achievement, culminating in her historic swim across the Straits of Florida - a testament to the indomitable spirit that was forged in the crucible of her Floridian childhood.

## Training and early competitions

Diana Nyad's life, a testament to unwavering determination and the relentless pursuit of dreams, was shaped from the earliest days by a powerful connection to the water. Born in 1949, her earliest memories were of the sun-drenched shores of Florida, where she developed a love for swimming that would define her future. This innate affinity wasn't simply a recreational pastime; it was a foundational element in her development, shaping her physical and mental fortitude, preparing her for challenges that would stretch the very limits of human endurance.

Her earliest competitive swims, though not necessarily grand feats, were critical in her nascent journey. She began with the familiar waters of the Coral Gables pool, a setting that not only introduced her to structured training but also to the thrill of competition. This initial experience fostered a competitive spirit that would grow stronger with each passing year, fueled by a desire to push beyond perceived limitations. It was during this formative stage that Nyad discovered a unique talent - an ability to stay afloat for extended periods with minimal effort. This innate gift, coupled with her intrinsic love for the water, became her most valuable assets, laying the foundation for future triumphs.

The Coral Gables pool, however, was merely the starting point. Soon, Nyad's aspirations took her beyond the familiar confines of her local pool. She began to compete in longer distances, the challenge of open water beckoning her. These early open water races, while seemingly insignificant in the grand narrative of her career, were crucial stepping stones, exposing her to the unforgiving elements of nature, the unpredictable currents, and the fatigue that comes with extended exposure.

One significant early competition, the 10-mile swim from Key West to Boca Chica, stands out as a pivotal moment. This event, while far from her ultimate ambitions, showcased a remarkable resilience in the face of physical and mental challenges. Despite battling against strong currents, Nyad persevered, finishing the race in a time that proved she was no ordinary swimmer. This experience, etched in her memory, became a benchmark, a testament to her ability to endure hardship, and an early indication of the indomitable spirit that would define her later achievements.

However, Nyad's competitive journey was not a seamless journey to victory. She encountered setbacks, moments of doubt, and challenges that threatened to derail her ambition. These setbacks, however, were not merely roadblocks; they were invaluable lessons. Each defeat, each moment of adversity, provided opportunities for reflection, for analyzing her strengths and weaknesses, for fine-tuning her training regimen. This willingness to learn from failures, to constantly adapt and improve, was a defining characteristic of Nyad's approach to swimming.

Training, for Nyad, was never just about building physical strength; it was a holistic approach encompassing mental discipline, endurance, and an understanding of the elements. She honed her swimming technique, meticulously perfecting her stroke, her breathing, and her rhythm. She trained tirelessly, pushing her limits, enduring physical discomfort, and cultivating an unwavering determination to succeed. This rigorous training regimen, fueled by her unwavering desire, laid the foundation for the exceptional endurance that would later allow her to conquer seemingly impossible challenges.

The early stages of Nyad's swimming journey were marked by a relentless pursuit of excellence, a relentless dedication to refining her skills and pushing her limits. While these early competitions may not have been the grand feats that would later define her career, they were essential building blocks, shaping her into the resilient, determined, and ultimately triumphant swimmer she would become. They laid the foundation, the groundwork for the extraordinary feats that would come to define her legacy: a testament to the power of perseverance, the allure of impossible dreams, and the unwavering pursuit of human potential.

## *Olympic dreams and setbacks*

Diana Nyad, the name evokes a sense of unwavering determination and resilience, a woman who dared to dream the impossible and pushed the boundaries of human endurance. Her life story is a testament to the power of the human spirit, a captivating narrative woven with threads of Olympic aspirations, crushing setbacks, and an unyielding pursuit of a singular goal. Nyad's early life and swimming journey were a crucible in which her formidable spirit was forged, shaping her into the legendary figure she is today.

Born in 1949, Diana Nyad's early life was a tapestry woven with the vibrant threads of Miami's sun-drenched beaches and the invigorating waters of the Atlantic Ocean. It was in this setting that her love for swimming blossomed, a love that would become a driving force in her life. From a young age, Nyad displayed an exceptional natural aptitude for the sport, gliding through the water with grace and power, her strokes seemingly effortless. The pool became her sanctuary, a place where she found solace and a sense of boundless possibility.

Her natural talent quickly garnered attention. In 1965, at the tender age of 16, Nyad achieved a remarkable feat by becoming the youngest swimmer ever to qualify for the US Olympic Trials. The national stage beckoned, and Nyad was brimming with youthful ambition, fueled by the dream of representing her country in the Olympics. However, the path to Olympic glory was not paved with smooth sailing. She fell agonizingly short of making the Olympic team, a setback that left her heartbroken and questioning her abilities.

This early disappointment, however, did not dampen her spirit. Nyad's unwavering determination burned brighter than ever, fueled by an inner fire that refused to be extinguished. She viewed the setback not as a defeat, but as a valuable lesson, a stepping stone on her journey. Nyad was already forging her own path, her sights set beyond the traditional confines of competitive swimming. .

Despite her dreams of Olympic glory fading, she continued her rigorous training. Her unwavering dedication to the sport manifested itself in a relentless pursuit of excellence. Nyad's ambition knew no bounds, her dreams extending beyond the traditional confines of the pool. She craved new challenges, pushing the limits of human endurance, an insatiable thirst for adventure driving her every move. This relentless drive, coupled with an unparalleled physical prowess, became the hallmark of her career, her unwavering belief in her abilities a beacon of hope for those who witnessed her journey.

Nyad's resilience, her unwavering belief in her abilities, were tested time and again. She was a pioneer in the world of open-water swimming, her early career marked by groundbreaking swims across the English Channel, the Straits of Gibraltar, and the Catalina Channel. She was a visionary, a trailblazer, forever pushing the boundaries of human endurance, her name becoming synonymous with daring feats of athleticism and unparalleled determination.

The pursuit of the impossible became Nyad's defining characteristic. She embraced challenges that others deemed insurmountable, her resilience tested time and again by the unforgiving forces of nature. She refused to be defined by setbacks, viewing them as opportunities for growth, as stepping stones on her relentless journey towards achieving the seemingly unattainable. .

Nyad's journey was punctuated by both triumphs and defeats, moments of exhilarating victory juxtaposed with the sting of crushing setbacks. The journey was arduous, requiring immense physical and mental fortitude, her commitment to her goals never wavering. She faced physical exhaustion, the relentless assault of the elements, and the gnawing doubts that crept into even the most determined mind. But through it all, she persevered, her spirit unyielding, driven by a burning desire to prove that the limits of human endurance were far greater than most dared to believe.

One of the most profound turning points in Nyad's career came in 1975, with her successful swim from Bimini to Florida, a grueling 52-mile journey that took her 27 hours to complete. This victory not only solidified her reputation as a world-class open-water swimmer but also served as a powerful catalyst for her future endeavors. It marked a shift in her focus, a turning point that propelled her towards a new level of ambition, her sights set on even greater challenges. .

As Nyad matured as an athlete, her ambition grew, her pursuit of the impossible taking her beyond the realm of competitive swimming. She began to envision feats that had never been accomplished, pushing the boundaries of human endurance to the extreme. Her aspirations transcended the confines of conventional sports, becoming a testament to the power of the human spirit, a testament to the indomitable nature of a woman who refused to be limited by the expectations of others.

Diana Nyad's journey was a testament to the power of dreams. Her early life and swimming journey were a crucible in which her extraordinary spirit was forged, an unwavering belief in her abilities, and a relentless pursuit of her goals. Her Olympic aspirations, though unfulfilled, served as a foundation upon which she built an extraordinary career, her pursuit of the impossible shaping her into a legendary figure whose achievements continue to inspire and amaze generations. . .

# Chapter 2: Around the World

## Embarking on a series of endurance swims

Diana Nyad's "The Pursuit of the Impossible" chronicles a life defined by pushing boundaries, particularly in the unforgiving realm of long-distance swimming. This book, a testament to human resilience, delves into Nyad's unwavering determination to conquer the seemingly insurmountable, embarking on a series of endurance swims that challenged both her physical limits and her inner strength. The narrative weaves together a tapestry of Nyad's experiences, highlighting the rigorous training, meticulous planning, and unwavering mental fortitude required to navigate the treacherous currents of the open ocean.

Nyad's early forays into endurance swimming were marked by a relentless pursuit of personal growth. The "Around the World" chapter paints a vivid portrait of her evolving relationship with the water, a journey that began with a childhood fascination and blossomed into an insatiable desire to test her limits. Each swim, from the 1975 Manhattan Island Marathon Swim to the 1979 attempt to circumnavigate the island of Manhattan, serves as a stepping stone, a building block in her relentless pursuit of the impossible. Each challenge pushed Nyad further, honing her physical and mental endurance, preparing her for the ultimate test: conquering the treacherous currents of the Florida Straits.

The chapter's central focus, however, lies in the meticulous planning and preparation for the 1978 attempt to swim from Bimini to Florida, a feat previously deemed impossible due to the relentless currents, unpredictable weather, and potential encounters with marine life. Nyad, however, viewed this challenge not as an insurmountable obstacle, but as a chance to push the boundaries of human potential. Her meticulous planning involved years of intense physical training, coupled with a rigorous mental conditioning program, culminating in a finely-tuned machine ready to face the unforgiving elements.

This preparation was not just about physical strength, but about mental resilience. The book delves into the depths of Nyad's mental approach, highlighting her unwavering faith in herself and her ability to overcome adversity. This mental fortitude, cultivated through years of rigorous training and countless hours spent battling both the elements and her own doubts, proved to be a crucial asset in the face of relentless currents, grueling hours in the water, and the ever-present threat of exhaustion.

Nyad's relentless drive was not born out of a thirst for glory, but from a burning desire to prove to herself, and to the world, that limitations were self-imposed. This unwavering belief in her own potential fueled her perseverance, allowing her to push beyond the perceived limits of human endurance, shattering preconceived notions and inspiring countless others to strive for their own impossible dreams.

The chapter unfolds like a high-stakes drama, chronicling the tense moments of the swim, the unpredictable nature of the ocean, and the relentless fight against exhaustion, both physical and mental. Nyad's account is not simply a record of her journey, but a poignant reflection on the complexities of human endeavor, the delicate balance between physical and mental strength, and the unwavering spirit that drives one to push beyond perceived limits.

In the end, despite the valiant effort and the meticulous planning, the attempt to swim from Bimini to Florida ended in disappointment. Yet, rather than viewing this setback as a failure, Nyad embraced it as a learning experience, using the lessons gained to further fuel her drive and refine her approach. The chapter serves as a testament to the power of resilience, a reminder that even in the face of adversity, the pursuit of the impossible can be a source of personal growth and profound satisfaction. .

This series of endurance swims, meticulously documented in "The Pursuit of the Impossible," serves as a powerful testament to the human spirit's ability to overcome seemingly insurmountable challenges. It is a story of relentless determination, meticulous planning, and unwavering belief in one's own potential, a story that inspires us to embrace our own impossible dreams and strive to push beyond the perceived limits of what we believe we can achieve.

## Crossing the English Channel and other iconic bodies of water

Diana Nyad's relentless pursuit of the impossible, chronicled in "The Pursuit of the Impossible," is a testament to the enduring power of the human spirit. It is a narrative woven with threads of grit, resilience, and an unwavering belief in the potential of the human body to conquer seemingly insurmountable challenges. This journey, however, is not solely defined by her victories, but also by the profound lessons she learned from her defeats..

Nyad's journey began with a childhood filled with water. Her early experiences in the ocean, a place she considered her "second home," instilled in her a profound sense of awe and an insatiable desire to explore its depths. This early immersion in the world of water fostered within her a unique blend of fearlessness and respect for the power of nature, a duality that would later become the cornerstone of her remarkable career..

The English Channel, a watery frontier that has beckoned adventurers for centuries, became the initial test of Nyad's mettle. Her first attempt, undertaken in 1975, ended in a harrowing experience, a reminder that the ocean's allure was not without its dangers. Nyad was forced to concede defeat, facing the relentless currents and a fierce internal struggle against the relentless assault of the waves. Yet, instead of succumbing to the sting of failure, she used it as a catalyst for growth, recognizing the need for meticulous preparation and an unwavering belief in her own capabilities.

Undeterred by her initial setback, Nyad returned to the Channel three years later, this time fueled by a burning desire for redemption. Her preparation was meticulous, a testament to her commitment to achieving her goals. The journey was a symphony of physical and mental fortitude, pushing her to the limits of human endurance. Ultimately, she emerged victorious, becoming the first woman to swim the Channel without a protective cage, a feat that cemented her place in the annals of long-distance swimming history.

But Nyad's journey did not end with the English Channel. Driven by an insatiable thirst for new challenges, she set her sights on other iconic bodies of water, each presenting its unique set of obstacles. From the treacherous waters of the Strait of Gibraltar, known for its strong currents and unpredictable tides, to the daunting waters of the Catalina Channel, notorious for its cold temperatures and unpredictable marine life, Nyad continued to test the limits of human endurance.

These journeys, while fraught with peril, offered Nyad a platform to explore the intricate relationship between the human spirit and the forces of nature. She learned to embrace the unpredictable, to find strength in the face of adversity, and to trust in the power of her own body to withstand the unrelenting demands of the open water.

Nyad's triumphs across these iconic bodies of water are not solely defined by the distance covered or the obstacles overcome. They are testaments to the indomitable spirit that resides within each of us, a spirit that can be ignited by the pursuit of a dream, fueled by a relentless determination, and sustained by a deep-seated belief in the impossible.

Her story, therefore, extends beyond the realm of athletic accomplishment. It is a profound exploration of the human potential, a testament to the power of resilience, and a reminder that the limits of the human spirit are defined not by the boundaries of the physical world, but by the boundaries we choose to set for ourselves.

# Exploring the world through swimming and advocacy

Diana Nyad's "Find a Way" ethos, born from her life-long passion for swimming, transcended mere athletic achievement, becoming a potent symbol of human potential and the transformative power of unwavering belief. Her journey, meticulously documented in "The Pursuit of the Impossible," showcases how swimming, beyond its physical demands, became a conduit for exploring the world and advocating for its preservation. Nyad's swims, often undertaken in treacherous conditions, were not merely feats of endurance but testaments to the human spirit's capacity to navigate the uncharted, both physically and metaphorically. She repeatedly pushed the boundaries of what was deemed possible, embodying a spirit of relentless pursuit and unyielding optimism that transcended the confines of the pool.

Each of Nyad's landmark swims - from her iconic Cuba-to-Florida journey to her marathon swims in the open ocean, often facing the daunting prospect of encountering dangerous marine life - was an exploration of the world's natural wonders. These swims were not just about conquering distance; they were about forging a deeper connection with the planet's vastness, experiencing its breathtaking beauty and confronting its perilous realities firsthand. From the crystal-clear waters of the Bahamas to the surging currents of the Atlantic, she dove into the heart of nature's raw power, revealing its magnificence and vulnerability simultaneously. These swims were not just athletic endeavors but acts of immersion, a testament to the profound connection between human spirit and the natural world.

Nyad's advocacy for ocean conservation emerged organically from these swims. Witnessing firsthand the impact of pollution and the escalating threats to marine ecosystems fueled her desire to become a voice for the voiceless. Recognizing the inextricable link between human well-being and the health of the oceans, she actively campaigned for environmental awareness, leveraging her platform to galvanize public support for sustainable practices. Her voice, amplified by her groundbreaking achievements, resonated with audiences across the globe, urging them to become stewards of the planet's precious marine resources.

The narrative of Nyad's swims, interwoven with her unwavering commitment to advocacy, paints a powerful picture of how athletic pursuits can transcend mere physical challenges. Her journey demonstrates that the pursuit of the impossible can not only inspire individuals to achieve the seemingly unattainable but also serve as a catalyst for positive change. By merging her passion for swimming with her dedication to environmental stewardship, Nyad created a legacy that extends far beyond the confines of competitive sport. Her story stands as a testament to the transformative power of human spirit, inspiring generations to embrace their own journeys of exploration, advocacy, and ultimately, a profound connection with the world around them. .

.

# Chapter 3: The Impossible Dream

## Contemplating the Cuba-Florida swim

Diana Nyad's "The Pursuit of the Impossible" is a compelling testament to the human spirit's ability to transcend seemingly insurmountable odds. Throughout the book, Nyad chronicles her lifelong pursuit of athletic excellence and her unwavering determination to achieve the seemingly impossible: swimming the 103-mile stretch from Cuba to Florida without a cage. Chapter 3, aptly titled "Contemplating the Cuba-Florida Swim," delves into the genesis of this audacious dream and provides crucial insight into the multifaceted challenges that Nyad anticipated confronting.

The chapter opens with Nyad recounting her childhood fascination with the sea and her early foray into competitive swimming. However, it's her encounter with the story of Cuban revolutionary leader, Antonio Maceo, that truly ignites the flame of ambition within her. Maceo's daring escape from Cuba to the United States by swimming across the treacherous Straits of Florida, a feat considered improbable by many, deeply resonated with Nyad's own yearning for adventure and the desire to push the boundaries of human endurance. This historical anecdote served as a powerful catalyst, planting the seed of the Cuba-Florida swim dream deep within her subconscious.

As Nyad matured, her love for the ocean deepened, and she began to explore the world through the lens of long-distance swimming. Her initial swims, though formidable, were merely stepping stones leading to the ultimate challenge: the Cuba-Florida crossing. Nyad, with her innate curiosity and thirst for knowledge, meticulously researched the historical attempts of others who had sought to conquer this formidable swim. The failures of previous attempts, including those of her own, fuelled her determination rather than deterring her. She dissected the reasons behind those failures, meticulously analyzing the confluence of factors that ultimately led to their demise, meticulously preparing for the day when she could confront the same challenges with a refined strategy and unwavering mental fortitude.

The chapter then delves into the inherent complexities of the Cuba-Florida swim. Nyad meticulously unpacks the myriad of factors that would conspire against her. She recognized that the Straits of Florida was not merely a body of water but a swirling vortex of dangers. The unpredictable currents, treacherous tides, and unpredictable weather patterns posed formidable obstacles to overcome. She acknowledged the omnipresent threat of jellyfish stings, the agonizing pain of which could easily derail her journey. Moreover, the sheer isolation of the swim, the immense physical exertion, and the constant threat of exhaustion presented formidable mental and physical barriers. The vast distance, the lack of a physical cage to protect her from marine life, and the constant threat of sharks in the surrounding waters heightened the perilous nature of her undertaking.

Yet, Nyad's relentless pursuit of this impossible dream was not borne out of a reckless disregard for danger but rather an insatiable thirst for pushing the boundaries of human potential. Her meticulously crafted plan, born out of extensive research and consultation with experts, was a testament to her calculated approach. She meticulously analyzed the historical attempts and failures, acknowledging the shortcomings of previous strategies, and formulating a meticulously crafted plan designed to mitigate the risks while maximizing her chances of success. She meticulously chose the optimal season for the swim, meticulously researching the prevailing currents and weather patterns during that time. Her meticulous preparations included extensive training regimens designed to enhance her physical and mental endurance, ensuring she was ready to confront the grueling demands of the journey.

Nyad's chapter is a testament to the power of a well-defined goal. The Cuba-Florida swim, a seemingly impossible dream, was meticulously transformed into a tangible aspiration. She painstakingly mapped out a strategy, meticulously outlining the steps needed to navigate the formidable challenges ahead. She envisioned the journey, meticulously anticipating the physical and mental hurdles she would need to overcome. Her meticulously crafted approach reflected the meticulous dedication and meticulous attention to detail that would characterize her entire journey.

The chapter culminates with Nyad's profound realization that the Cuba-Florida swim was not merely a physical feat but a journey of self-discovery. She acknowledged that the swim represented a profound exploration of the limits of human endurance, a testament to the resilience of the human spirit. She understood that the journey was not just about the destination, but about the transformative power of confronting one's fears, pushing beyond perceived limitations, and embracing the inherent potential within. .

Nyad's "Contemplating the Cuba-Florida Swim" is a captivating exploration of the human spirit's ability to dream big, to relentlessly pursue the impossible, and to redefine what's considered achievable. It's a testament to the transformative power of facing one's fears, pushing beyond perceived limitations, and embracing the inherent potential within. The chapter lays the groundwork for Nyad's ultimate journey, a testament to the power of meticulous preparation, unwavering dedication, and an unyielding belief in oneself.

## Training for the extreme challenge

Diana Nyad's pursuit of swimming the Florida Straits, a daunting 110-mile journey across treacherous waters, demanded not just physical prowess but a level of mental fortitude seldom seen. Her training was not merely a physical preparation, but a rigorous mental and spiritual conditioning for the ultimate test of human endurance.

Nyad's training wasn't a linear process; it was a dynamic, ever-evolving tapestry woven with resilience, adaptability, and relentless self-belief. The book underscores the significance of her initial journey, a 1975 attempt that ended prematurely due to a jellyfish sting. This early failure, rather than extinguishing her ambition, fueled her fire. It served as a crucible, forging her determination and shaping her training for future endeavors. This initial experience birthed a profound understanding of the ocean's capricious nature, a respect that would guide her subsequent preparations.

The training for her 2013 attempt, at the age of 64, mirrored her age, seasoned with wisdom and experience. It was a meticulous process encompassing not just physical endurance, but also mental and psychological conditioning. Nyad immersed herself in an elaborate routine, driven by the belief that the key to conquering the impossible lies in the ability to push beyond perceived limitations.

Her physical regimen was as demanding as the journey itself. Daily swims of up to 10,000 yards in open waters, braving the cold, unpredictable conditions of the Atlantic Ocean, became the cornerstone of her preparation. These intense swims pushed her body to its limits, building muscle strength, cardiovascular endurance, and a tolerance for the unforgiving elements. Nyad's dedication was unwavering, as she meticulously analyzed every stroke, every breath, striving for optimal efficiency to conserve energy for the grueling marathon swim.

But Nyad's approach was not limited to brute force. She recognized that the mental aspect was equally crucial. The book vividly depicts her exploration of meditative practices, a conscious effort to train her mind to withstand the inevitable onslaught of doubt and fear that would accompany her journey. Meditation became her anchor, a tool to achieve inner peace, cultivate focus, and build resilience against the relentless mental battle that lay ahead. .

Alongside physical training, Nyad meticulously prepared for the unique challenges presented by the Florida Straits. Her team conducted extensive research, analyzing currents, weather patterns, and the presence of marine life, particularly jellyfish. Nyad herself underwent rigorous training in the use of a custom-made full-body swimsuit, designed to protect her from the stinging tentacles of jellyfish. The knowledge gleaned from this research and the meticulous planning that followed were instrumental in mitigating the risks associated with the swim.

Nyad's preparation was not simply about physical endurance, but also about cultivating an unwavering belief in her ability to succeed. The book showcases her unwavering commitment to the pursuit of her dream, highlighting the countless hours she spent visualizing the swim, mentally rehearsing every stage of the journey, and affirming her resolve. This mental preparation, alongside her physical training, became a powerful arsenal against the insidious whispers of doubt that threatened to derail her mission.

The book further emphasizes Nyad's reliance on her support team, a vital aspect of her training. The team consisted of experts in marine biology, navigation, and medical support, each contributing their unique expertise to ensure her safety and success. Nyad's ability to trust her team implicitly, to acknowledge their strengths and rely on their expertise, became a crucial pillar in her preparation. This trust allowed her to focus her energy on her own physical and mental fortitude, knowing that she was surrounded by a dedicated team ready to support her every step of the way.

Nyad's training was not simply about preparing for a physical challenge; it was about preparing for an emotional and spiritual journey. The book delves into her personal struggles, her moments of doubt, and her unwavering commitment to her dream. These accounts reveal the raw human vulnerability behind the extraordinary feat she was about to undertake. Nyad's training was about harnessing the power of her human spirit, her resilience, her unwavering belief in the power of the human will to overcome seemingly impossible odds.

It was not merely a physical preparation but a comprehensive approach encompassing physical, mental, and emotional training. Nyad's journey serves as an inspiration, a reminder that the human spirit, fueled by unwavering belief, can overcome any obstacle.

## *Facing criticism and skepticism*

Diana Nyad's pursuit of swimming from Cuba to Florida was a monumental challenge, not just physically, but also mentally and emotionally. While the world marveled at her ambition, she also faced a torrent of criticism and skepticism, fueled by a combination of factors: the sheer impossibility of the feat, doubts about her age, and the historical failures of others who had attempted the same. .

The first wave of skepticism stemmed from the very nature of her goal. Swimming 103 miles in treacherous waters, with open ocean currents, jellyfish stings, and the ever-present threat of sharks, was seen by many as an impossible feat. Experts, including seasoned ocean swimmers, raised serious concerns about the physical limitations of the human body, arguing that such a distance was simply beyond reach. The daunting nature of the challenge, coupled with the lack of historical precedent for a successful solo swim of this scale, further fueled the doubts. .

Even within the swimming community, Nyad's ambition was met with raised eyebrows. Many questioned her decision to attempt the swim at the age of 64, considering it a foolhardy pursuit for someone well past their athletic prime. The physical demands of such an endeavor, they argued, were too great for someone of her age. While Nyad acknowledged the challenges of her age, she countered the criticism with unwavering determination, emphasizing her mental strength and years of rigorous training. .

Adding to the skepticism was the history of failed attempts. Others before her, including the legendary marathon swimmer, Susie Maroney, had tried and failed to conquer the Cuba-Florida swim. These setbacks further solidified the perception that the feat was simply beyond human capability, casting a shadow of doubt on Nyad's own aspirations. .

The media, often eager for a dramatic narrative, capitalized on the skepticism, presenting a public image of Nyad as an aging, reckless dreamer, destined to fail. Headlines like "Nyad's Dream Run Amok" and

"The Impossible Swim" reinforced the prevailing skepticism, painting her as a delusional figure clinging to a futile ambition.

However, Nyad remained undeterred. Instead of succumbing to the negativity, she channeled the skepticism into fuel for her determination. She used it as a motivation to prove her doubters wrong, to demonstrate that age and past failures were not insurmountable obstacles.

This defiance, coupled with her unwavering belief in her own capabilities, allowed her to push past the limitations that others had placed upon her. Her journey became a testament to the power of human will and the potential to break through perceived barriers.

Nyad's triumph in 2013, after a decade of relentless pursuit, was a victory not only for herself, but also for the human spirit. It silenced the skeptics and redefined the boundaries of human achievement.

More than just a physical feat, Nyad's journey embodied the power of perseverance, the strength of the human will, and the ability to overcome adversity. It challenged the limits of what was considered possible, inspiring others to pursue their own dreams, no matter how improbable they may seem.

# Chapter 4: The First Attempt (2011)

## Attempting the swim with a team of 33

The chapter, "The First Attempt," unveils a pivotal moment in Diana Nyad's relentless pursuit of conquering the Florida Straits. The year is 2011, and Nyad, seasoned by years of swimming and a prior attempt in 1978, embarks on this grueling endeavor with an assembled team of 33. This meticulously chosen team, a symphony of expertise and dedication, becomes the bedrock of her ambitious undertaking. Their roles are meticulously defined, each member contributing their unique skill set to ensure Nyad's safety and success..

Nyad's team is a microcosm of the challenges she faces. It encompasses experienced maritime professionals, expert navigators, dedicated medical staff, and seasoned support crew. These individuals, each driven by Nyad's unwavering spirit, form a unified force dedicated to her mission. Their presence is a testament to the sheer magnitude of the undertaking. Each member is aware that Nyad's physical strength and mental resilience are not the only factors determining the outcome. The unforgiving ocean, unpredictable currents, and the potential for marine life encounters demand a comprehensive support system..

The chapter reveals the meticulous planning that precedes Nyad's plunge into the water. The team meticulously studies the currents, mapping the flow patterns and identifying potential danger zones. They meticulously research the marine life that inhabits the Straits, considering potential encounters with sharks and other creatures. The team meticulously designs a strategy to navigate the treacherous waters, factoring in the unpredictable nature of the ocean environment.

The chapter portrays the logistical complexities of the mission. The team, armed with cutting-edge technology, monitors Nyad's progress throughout her swim. Sophisticated tracking systems provide real-time data on her location, speed, and physiological parameters. The team, with their vast expertise, monitors weather conditions, constantly evaluating potential risks. They understand the ocean's unpredictable nature, and their vigilance is crucial to Nyad's safety..

Nyad's team isn't merely a collection of individuals; they become an extended family, bound by their shared goal. Their collective strength and unwavering support, combined with their expertise, provide Nyad with the necessary foundation to tackle the daunting task before her. This unified force, a testament to the power of human collaboration, underscores the critical role of teamwork in Nyad's quest to conquer the Florida Straits..

## Facing jellyfish stings and strong currents

Diana Nyad, a legendary long-distance swimmer, embarked on a remarkable journey to conquer the seemingly impossible: a solo, non-stop swim from Cuba to Florida..

Nyad's first attempt in 2011, though ultimately unsuccessful, served as a crucial learning experience, revealing the brutal reality of her undertaking. From the outset, the ocean presented a relentless assault. The pervasive presence of jellyfish, their venomous tentacles capable of inflicting excruciating pain, posed a constant threat. Nyad's team, equipped with specialized suits designed to deter these stinging creatures, meticulously monitored the water, strategically guiding her path to minimize exposure. However, despite these precautions, Nyad found herself repeatedly stung, enduring the agonizing pain with remarkable resilience..

The relentless currents, a force of nature that could easily derail her progress, proved to be another formidable adversary. Nyad and her team meticulously studied oceanographic data, meticulously planning her route to minimize the impact of strong currents. Yet, the unpredictable nature of the ocean constantly challenged their calculations. As Nyad plunged into the water, the currents relentlessly tugged at her, testing her strength and endurance. The vastness of the ocean, the relentless currents, and the constant threat of jellyfish stings combined to create a daunting and overwhelming environment.

Nyad's 2011 attempt was a testament to her determination and tenacity, but it also underscored the harsh realities of her endeavor. The ocean, a formidable and unforgiving adversary, presented a constant threat, demanding every ounce of her physical and mental strength. The agonizing pain of jellyfish stings and the relentless push of the currents underscored the immense challenges she faced. This initial failure, however, did not deter Nyad. Instead, it served as a powerful catalyst, fueling her determination to overcome the obstacles that had thwarted her attempt. She meticulously analyzed the factors that led to her early exit, meticulously refining her strategies and preparations for future endeavors. The experience provided invaluable lessons, shaping her approach and strengthening her resolve. .

As Nyad reflects upon her first attempt, she acknowledges the humbling nature of her experience. She recognizes the immense power of the ocean, its ability to defy human control and impose its will. The relentless stings, the relentless currents, and the overwhelming sense of isolation served as powerful reminders of the sheer scale of her challenge. Yet, through this adversity, Nyad discovered a strength she never knew she possessed, a resilience that would ultimately guide her towards her ultimate triumph.

.

## Decision to end the attempt

The decision to end her first attempt, a pivotal moment in Diana Nyad's relentless pursuit of the impossible, was a confluence of factors, each chipping away at her resolve, each a testament to the grueling nature of the challenge. Nyad's body, a testament to her unwavering spirit, had endured a barrage of hardships. Jellyfish stings, a constant presence in the warm waters, had become a relentless tormentor, leaving her skin raw and inflamed. The stings were not merely a physical discomfort; they were a constant reminder of the unforgiving environment that surrounded her, a constant reminder that the ocean was not a playground for her audacious dream. .

The persistent stings, however, were not the only challenge that Nyad faced. Fatigue, a natural consequence of her relentless effort, began to take its toll. Her body, pushed to its limits, started to betray her. Every stroke, every kick, became a struggle, demanding a Herculean effort that her body could no longer sustain. Sleep deprivation, another consequence of her relentless pursuit, added to the burden. The lack of restful sleep left her mentally and physically drained, her focus becoming clouded by the fog of exhaustion. .

The looming threat of storms, a constant specter in the open ocean, was a major factor in Nyad's decision. The unpredictable nature of the weather, a force she could not control, was a constant source of anxiety, threatening to derail her attempt. The knowledge that a powerful storm was approaching, a force capable of turning the ocean into a maelstrom, weighed heavily on her mind. The knowledge that she could be swept away by the storm, her dream shattered by the capricious whims of nature, was a risk she could not afford. .

But perhaps the most poignant factor in Nyad's decision was the growing realization that she was simply not prepared for the magnitude of the challenge. Her training, while rigorous, had not adequately prepared her for the specific demands of this swim. She had underestimated the impact of the currents, the unforgiving nature of the open ocean, and the unrelenting physical and mental toll it would take. She had underestimated the relentless force of the ocean, the endless fight against the elements, the constant battle against the relentless forces of nature. .

The decision to end the attempt was a painful one, a testament to her unwavering commitment to self-preservation. It was a recognition that sometimes, even the most determined spirit must acknowledge the limits of *human endurance. This was not a failure but a necessary step, a moment of introspection that allowed her to learn from her experience and prepare for the next attempt, a testament to her relentless pursuit of the impossible.*

## Chapter 5: Recovery and Rededication

### Reflecting on the failure and rebuilding strength

Diana Nyad's relentless pursuit of swimming the Florida Straits, culminating in her historic achievement at the age of 64, stands as a testament to human resilience and the enduring power of the human spirit. However, her journey was far from a smooth sail, punctuated by a series of setbacks that threatened to extinguish her dream altogether. These failures, rather than crushing her spirit, served as potent catalysts for introspection and reinvention, propelling her towards the monumental feat she ultimately conquered. .

Nyad's first attempt in 1978 ended prematurely when a severe storm forced her out of the water. This initial setback served as a rude awakening, revealing the unforgiving nature of the open ocean and the sheer magnitude of the challenge she had undertaken. It also instilled in her a deep respect for the power of nature, a respect that would guide her future endeavors. .

The subsequent attempts, spanning over three decades, were marred by a series of challenges that pushed Nyad to her physical and mental limits. The constant threat of jellyfish stings, the unrelenting currents, the fatigue that threatened to engulf her, and the crushing weight of her own self-doubt relentlessly tested her resolve. Each failure, however, served as a valuable learning experience, forcing her to confront her weaknesses, adapt her strategies, and strengthen her resolve.

The 2012 attempt, a monumental undertaking in itself, ultimately ended in failure due to a severe bout of jellyfish stings. This setback, though deeply painful, proved to be a turning point in Nyad's journey. The experience forced her to confront her own mortality, her physical limitations, and the enduring power of her own spirit. .

Instead of succumbing to despair, Nyad used this setback as an opportunity for introspection and reevaluation. She sought guidance from experts in the fields of marine biology, jellyfish research, and physical conditioning. She meticulously analyzed the previous attempts, identifying patterns, weaknesses, and areas for improvement. This period of reflection was marked by a profound sense of determination, a refusal to be defeated by the seemingly insurmountable odds stacked against her.

Nyad's ultimate success in 2013, after a series of painstakingly planned attempts, wasn't solely a triumph of physical endurance. It was the culmination of a profound journey of self-discovery, a relentless pursuit of personal growth, and a testament to the power of the human spirit to rise above adversity. The failures she endured along the way, far from crippling her, served as the bedrock of her resilience, fueling her determination and pushing her to the very edge of her capabilities. .

The narrative of Nyad's journey underscores the paradoxical nature of failure. It is often seen as a sign of weakness, a blemish on one's record. However, Nyad's story demonstrates the transformative power of failure, its ability to become a catalyst for growth, innovation, and ultimately, triumph. By embracing her setbacks, Nyad was able to learn from them, adapt, and ultimately achieve the impossible. Her story stands as a testament to the indomitable spirit within us all, a reminder that even in the face of seemingly insurmountable odds, the human spirit can rise above adversity, emerge stronger, and ultimately achieve the extraordinary. .

## Training with a new team and strategy

The fifth chapter of Diana Nyad's captivating memoir, "The Pursuit of the Impossible," marks a pivotal turning point in her arduous journey to conquer the treacherous waters of the Florida Straits. Having faced the crushing weight of failure in her previous attempts, Nyad found herself at a crossroads. Her spirit, though bruised, remained unbroken. The burning desire to achieve her lifelong dream, to swim from Cuba to Florida without a cage, still flickered within her. However, she knew that a complete overhaul was necessary, both physically and strategically.

This chapter serves as a testament to Nyad's unwavering determination, her willingness to embrace change, and her ability to learn from setbacks. The narrative delves into the meticulous process of assembling a new team, a process that reflected her deep understanding of the complexities of long-distance swimming. She meticulously handpicked individuals, each with unique expertise, to form a cohesive unit dedicated to supporting her in this daunting endeavor..

Nyad's previous team, though well-intentioned, lacked the specific skillsets required for a successful Florida Straits swim. This realization, born out of the harsh lessons learned from past failures, prompted a complete overhaul. She recognized the need for a diverse team that encompassed not only technical prowess but also unwavering mental support..

The narrative meticulously details the selection process, highlighting the importance of each member's role. Nyad sought a team physician with extensive experience in endurance sports, someone who could meticulously monitor her physical well-being throughout the grueling swim. Her search led her to Dr. Brendan McQuillan, a specialist in sports medicine, whose expertise in optimizing performance and mitigating risks proved invaluable..

In addition to a skilled physician, Nyad knew she needed a team that could effectively navigate the treacherous waters. She sought an experienced navigator, someone who could meticulously map the unpredictable currents and provide real-time guidance during the swim. She found her answer in Bonnie Stoll, a seasoned oceanographer with a deep understanding of the Florida Straits. Stoll's expertise in ocean currents and weather patterns became a vital asset, enabling Nyad to strategize and adjust her route based on ever-changing environmental conditions.

The team's composition extended beyond medical and navigational expertise. Nyad recognized the crucial need for a dedicated support crew, individuals who could provide unwavering emotional and practical assistance throughout the challenge. She sought individuals who possessed the resilience to withstand the pressures of long-distance swims, individuals who could provide a steady hand during moments of doubt and fatigue..

The chapter meticulously chronicles the process of assembling this crucial support team, highlighting the diverse skillsets and personal qualities that Nyad sought. She sought individuals who possessed a deep understanding of swimming dynamics, individuals who could effectively manage logistics and communicate clearly under pressure..

The narrative highlights the importance of teamwork, emphasizing how Nyad's meticulous approach to assembling this team was integral to her eventual success. Her ability to delegate tasks, to foster a collaborative environment, and to recognize the strengths of each individual contributed significantly to the team's overall effectiveness.

Beyond the team composition, the chapter delves into Nyad's meticulous focus on refining her training strategy. She knew that the grueling swim required not only physical endurance but also mental fortitude. She sought a training regimen that would push her to her limits, a regimen that would prepare her to face the relentless waves, the unpredictable currents, and the mental fatigue inherent in such an arduous challenge.

Nyad's training program was designed to mimic the conditions she would encounter in the Florida Straits, incorporating drills that focused on building endurance, strengthening core muscles, and enhancing her ability to withstand the unforgiving conditions. She spent countless hours in the open ocean, simulating the long swims she would endure, conditioning her body to adapt to the varying temperatures, the constant motion of the waves, and the physical demands of battling currents.

Her training program went beyond the physical realm. She recognized the critical role of mental resilience in overcoming the challenges of long-distance swimming. She sought to develop her mental strength, to cultivate a mindset that could withstand the inevitable moments of doubt and despair. She sought strategies to stay focused, to maintain a positive attitude, and to draw strength from her own internal reserves.

Nyad's training program was a reflection of her deep understanding of the psychology of endurance. She sought to cultivate a mental toughness that could withstand the physical and emotional toll of a grueling swim. She understood that achieving her goal would require not only physical strength but also the unwavering belief that she could conquer the seemingly impossible.

The chapter reveals the profound impact of Nyad's new team and training strategy, highlighting their contribution to her renewed sense of confidence and purpose. She found in her team a source of unwavering support, a network of individuals who believed in her vision and who were dedicated to helping her achieve her dreams. Her training program not only honed her physical abilities but also reinforced her mental fortitude, equipping her to face the challenges that lay ahead.

This pivotal chapter in "The Pursuit of the Impossible" paints a vivid portrait of Nyad's resilience and her unwavering commitment to her dream. It showcases her ability to learn from setbacks, to adapt her strategies, and to assemble a team that would provide the support she needed to face the daunting task ahead. The chapter underscores the importance of both physical and mental preparation in achieving seemingly impossible feats, offering a profound reminder of the power of human resilience.

# Chapter 6: The Second Attempt (2012)

## Setting out again with a modified approach

The sting of failure, though bitter, can be the catalyst for a renewed and refined pursuit. Diana Nyad's first attempt to swim from Cuba to Florida, a 110-mile odyssey through treacherous waters, ended in defeat. The relentless currents, the menacing jellyfish, and the gnawing fatigue had proven too much for even her indomitable spirit. But failure did not extinguish her ambition; it ignited a desire to learn, to adapt, and to conquer the impossible.

The second attempt, a testament to Nyad's unwavering resolve and her willingness to learn from her mistakes, was a meticulously planned and strategically executed mission. The culmination of months of intense preparation, rigorous training, and an in-depth analysis of the oceanic environment, it reflected a deep understanding of the ocean's capricious nature. Recognizing the impact of the Loop Current on her previous journey, Nyad, alongside her team, meticulously studied the currents, identifying patterns and weaknesses. They painstakingly charted the optimal route, taking into account the ebb and flow of the waters, seeking a path that would minimize the impact of the relentless currents. .

The second attempt was not merely a replication of the first. It was a refined strategy, a meticulously crafted plan based on the hard-won lessons of defeat. Nyad, in collaboration with her team, had carefully studied the data from the first attempt, meticulously analyzing the factors that led to her unsuccessful completion. The grueling training regimen, designed to prepare her body and mind for the rigors of the journey, took on a new dimension, incorporating the lessons learned from the first attempt. Her team, a collection of seasoned experts, brought an array of skills to the table - from navigation and oceanography to physical therapy and mental coaching. They were not merely support personnel; they were an integral part of the intricate strategy, each member contributing their expertise to ensure a successful outcome.

Central to Nyad's approach was the understanding that the journey was as much a mental battle as a physical one. This realization, born from the harsh realities of her first attempt, led to the incorporation of mindfulness techniques into her training. She spent hours meditating, learning to control her thoughts, and harnessing the power of her inner strength. This mental preparation, coupled with the physical endurance she honed, formed the cornerstone of her strategy. The ability to withstand the relentless physical demands of the swim while simultaneously maintaining a calm, focused mind became the key to her success.

The second attempt was marked by a profound sense of purpose, a deep-seated determination that transcended the mere pursuit of athletic accomplishment. Nyad's motivation stemmed from a desire to push the boundaries of human endurance, to prove that even the most daunting challenges could be overcome with unwavering resolve and a carefully crafted strategy. The lessons learned from her first attempt had not only honed her physical capabilities but had also cultivated a deeper understanding of her own mental fortitude. The second attempt was not simply a swim; it was a testament to the human spirit's capacity for resilience, adaptation, and unwavering determination.

The new strategy, built upon the foundation of the first attempt's lessons, was a testament to Nyad's unwavering commitment to learning and growth. The meticulous planning, the comprehensive training regimen, and the inclusion of mindfulness techniques were all manifestations of her deep desire to overcome the challenges that had thwarted her previous endeavor. Each aspect of the second attempt was designed to minimize the impact of the obstacles she had encountered before, reflecting a meticulous understanding of her limitations and a steadfast resolve to overcome them. The second attempt, a testament to the power of self-reflection and strategic adaptation, was more than just a swim; it was a journey of personal growth, a testament to the human spirit's capacity for resilience and unwavering determination.

## *Overcoming jellyfish bites and exhaustion*

The sixth chapter of Diana Nyad's The Pursuit of the Impossible delves into the harrowing experience of her second attempt to swim the Florida Straits, a grueling 110-mile journey from Cuba to Key West. This chapter, titled "The Second Attempt," is a testament to Nyad's resilience and unwavering determination in the face of insurmountable odds..

Nyad's 2012 attempt, undertaken at the age of 64, was fueled by a decade-long pursuit of a dream she had nurtured since her youth. Despite the seemingly impossible task, Nyad's resolve was unwavering, propelled by an insatiable thirst for adventure and a burning desire to achieve what many deemed impossible.

The chapter lays bare the relentless challenges that Nyad encountered during her swim. The Florida Straits, a notorious body of water teeming with marine life, presented a formidable obstacle. Jellyfish, particularly the venomous box jellyfish, were a constant threat. Nyad's team, acutely aware of this danger, meticulously researched the migration patterns of the creatures and strategized around their movements..

However, despite the meticulous planning, Nyad faced a relentless onslaught of jellyfish stings. The chapter describes the excruciating pain, the swelling, and the constant fear of encountering the potentially fatal box jellyfish. Nyad's resolve, however, remained unshaken. She endured the stinging agony, pushing herself to the brink of her physical and mental limits..

Nyad's resilience was further tested by the relentless fatigue that came with swimming for days on end. The chapter captures the toll that relentless exertion took on her body, the aching muscles, the blurry vision, and the exhaustion that threatened to overwhelm her..

But even amidst the physical and mental anguish, Nyad's determination refused to waver. She drew strength from the unwavering support of her team, the camaraderie of her fellow swimmers, and the enduring spirit that had driven her through countless hardships throughout her life. .

The chapter vividly portrays the psychological toll that the relentless challenges took on Nyad. The constant fear of jellyfish stings, the ever-present threat of exhaustion, and the isolation of being surrounded by vast stretches of open ocean all contributed to a relentless mental strain. .

Nyad's response to this psychological pressure is a testament to the strength of her character. The chapter reveals her internal struggle, the moments of doubt and despair, and the unwavering commitment that propelled her forward. .

The chapter culminates in Nyad's decision to abandon the second attempt. Despite the immense efforts she had poured into the swim, she realized that the conditions were too dangerous to proceed. This realization, while undoubtedly painful, was a testament to Nyad's wisdom and her unwavering commitment to her own safety. .

The chapter, while chronicling a failed attempt, does not convey defeat. It instead serves as a powerful reminder of Nyad's unwavering spirit, her ability to rise above even the most daunting challenges, and her indomitable will to persevere in the face of adversity. .

"The Second Attempt" chapter is a captivating journey into the depths of human determination, highlighting Nyad's resilience in the face of unimaginable pain, relentless exhaustion, and the constant threat of danger. The chapter underscores the complex interplay between physical strength and mental fortitude, showcasing the power of human spirit to overcome even the seemingly insurmountable obstacles. It stands as a compelling testament to Nyad's unwavering commitment to her dream, even in the face of relentless obstacles. .

## *Success after 53 hours of swimming*

The sun, a burning, malevolent eye in the Florida sky, bore down on Diana Nyad as she finally reached the beach at Key West. The world blurred, a kaleidoscope of swirling sand, sweat, and tears as she stumbled from the water, the culmination of years of tireless dedication and a lifetime of overcoming adversity. The accomplishment was monumental, a testament to the human spirit's unyielding capacity for resilience and a symbol of what can be achieved when passion and purpose ignite a single, unwavering flame.

53 hours. Fifty-three hours of relentless battle against the elements, the relentless pull of the Gulf Stream, and the constant threat of fatigue, jellyfish stings, and the ever-present danger of sharks. It was a journey that tested not only her physical endurance, but also her mental fortitude and the very essence of her being. The crushing weight of failure, the agonizing memory of her previous attempt, the relentless doubts that gnawed at her resolve, all threatened to extinguish the flickering flame of hope. Yet, Nyad refused to yield.

The years that followed her first attempt in 1978 were marked by a constant undercurrent of yearning, a persistent whisper that urged her back to the water, back to the open ocean, back to the challenge that had both consumed and liberated her. It was not simply a desire to conquer the distance, to prove to herself and to the world that it was possible. It was a yearning for redemption, a need to erase the bitter sting of defeat and to finally find peace with her own unwavering ambition.

Time and again, Nyad felt the pull of the ocean, the yearning to push her limits, to test the boundaries of what was deemed possible. She trained relentlessly, pushing her body to the edge of its limits, refusing to allow the relentless march of time to extinguish her passion. But the ocean, like a fickle lover, remained elusive, teasing her with its beauty and its promise while simultaneously reminding her of its formidable power.

The years between 1978 and 2012 were marked by setbacks, by moments of doubt and despair. But they were also marked by unwavering resilience, by a fierce determination that refused to be extinguished. The flame of her ambition, once nearly extinguished by the harsh winds of adversity, now burned brighter than ever, fueled by an internal fire that was both consuming and liberating.

The 2012 attempt was different. It was not simply about conquering a distance, it was about conquering the doubts, the fears, and the ghosts of her past. She surrounded herself with a team of experts, each playing a crucial role in the intricate dance of her attempt. The knowledge gleaned from her previous attempt, the advancements in technology, and the unwavering support of her team provided her with the confidence and the tools necessary to face the formidable challenge ahead.

The journey, however, was far from easy. The relentless pull of the Gulf Stream, the sting of jellyfish, and the ever-present threat of sharks served as constant reminders of the immense power of nature. The mental toll was equally taxing, the relentless battle against fatigue, the constant fear of failure, and the weight of expectations weighing heavily on her shoulders. Yet, Nyad persisted, drawing strength from the unwavering support of her team, the memory of past struggles, and the unshakeable belief in her own abilities.

On that final stretch, as she saw the lights of Key West shimmering in the distance, a wave of emotion washed over her. It was not simply relief or euphoria, but a profound sense of fulfillment, a validation of years of sacrifice and dedication. The world watched as she emerged from the water, a symbol of resilience, a testament to the power of human ambition, and a living embodiment of the impossible made possible.

The moment, however, was not just about a single individual. It was a moment of collective triumph, a celebration of the human spirit's ability to rise above adversity, to challenge the boundaries of what is deemed possible, and to inspire others to embrace their own dreams. Diana Nyad's journey, from the crushing disappointment of failure to the triumphant *moment of success, served as a beacon of hope, reminding us that even the most seemingly impossible dreams can be achieved with unwavering determination, a relentless spirit, and the unwavering belief in the power of human potential. .*

.

# Chapter 7: Triumph and Legacy

## The historic accomplishment and its impact

Diana Nyad's monumental swim from Cuba to Florida, achieved in 2013 at the age of 64, stands as a testament to human resilience, unwavering determination, and the boundless potential of the human spirit. Her triumph shattered the boundaries of what was considered possible in long-distance swimming, not only for a woman of her age, but for anyone. This wasn't merely a physical feat; it was a monumental act of courage, willpower, and self-belief, a beacon of inspiration that transcended the realm of sport and resonated with individuals around the globe.

Nyad's pursuit of this audacious dream, spanning over three decades, embodied the spirit of "the impossible" and fueled her unwavering drive. She had first attempted the Cuba-Florida swim in 1978, facing a grueling 53 hours in the water before succumbing to jellyfish stings and exhaustion. Undeterred, she continued to train relentlessly, honing her body and mind, preparing for the daunting challenges that lay ahead. Her persistence, fueled by a deep-seated belief in her ability to overcome obstacles, serves as a powerful reminder that with unwavering commitment, even the most formidable challenges can be conquered. .

Nyad's historic accomplishment shattered the prevailing notion that such feats were only attainable by younger, physically superior individuals. She boldly challenged the ageist and gendered assumptions that pervaded the world of endurance sports, proving that age, gender, and physical limitations were mere constructs that could be transcended through sheer willpower and determination. Her triumph became a symbol of hope for countless individuals who had been discouraged by societal limitations and the constraints of age, inspiring them to chase their own seemingly impossible dreams.

Beyond the individual triumph, Nyad's accomplishment reverberated across the global stage, igniting a wave of inspiration and igniting the imaginations of people from all walks of life. Her story became a powerful narrative, a testament to the potential that lies within each of us to achieve extraordinary things. It transcended the boundaries of sport and resonated with individuals seeking motivation and encouragement to overcome their own personal challenges.

Her impact extended beyond the world of athletics, touching upon themes of resilience, determination, and human potential. The media frenzy surrounding her swim brought the world's attention to the extraordinary feats that ordinary people could achieve when driven by a powerful purpose. Her success resonated with individuals of all ages and backgrounds, fueling their own dreams and aspirations. It served as a powerful reminder that the limits we impose on ourselves are often far less restrictive than the limitations we believe society has placed upon us.

Nyad's accomplishment, however, was not solely defined by the physical triumph. It also carried profound implications for the world of long-distance swimming. Her successful swim, accomplished without the aid of a protective cage, challenged the established safety protocols and highlighted the potential of the human body to endure extreme conditions. It paved the way for future generations of swimmers to push the boundaries of what was considered possible, inspiring them to dream bigger and explore the limits of human endurance.

Furthermore, Nyad's success provided a platform for addressing critical environmental issues. The challenges she faced, from jellyfish stings to harsh currents, brought attention to the fragility of our oceans and the impact of pollution on marine life. Her story became a catalyst for environmental awareness, prompting discussions about the need for ocean conservation and the importance of safeguarding this vital resource.

Diana Nyad's journey, from her initial attempts to her ultimate triumph, epitomizes the very essence of the human spirit, highlighting the transformative power of unwavering determination, the courage to break free from societal limitations, and the enduring legacy of pushing the boundaries of what is considered possible. Her accomplishment, etched into the annals of human achievement, serves as a timeless testament to the indomitable nature of the human spirit, a beacon of inspiration for generations to come. Nyad's legacy transcends the realm of sport, extending into the hearts and minds of countless individuals who have been empowered by her story, embracing the potential for greatness that lies within each of us. . .

## Inspiring others with her determination

It's a testament to the boundless potential of human spirit, a beacon of hope that shines brightest when faced with seemingly insurmountable obstacles. Nyad's unwavering determination, a driving force throughout her life, resonates with readers far beyond the realm of sports and outdoors. Her story is not just about conquering the physical challenges of swimming across the treacherous Florida Straits, it's about the relentless pursuit of a dream, the refusal to be defined by limitations, and the inspiring belief that anything is possible with unyielding resolve.

Her determination, a constant companion throughout her life, is the defining thread woven through every chapter of her story. From her early days as a competitive swimmer, fueled by a fiery ambition to excel, to her later years where she faced the daunting prospect of swimming across the Florida Straits, an arduous journey previously conquered by only one person, Nyad's drive remained undeterred. This unwavering determination is not merely a trait; it's a philosophy, a guiding principle that fueled her pursuit of the seemingly impossible. . .

Nyad's first attempt at swimming across the Florida Straits, a feat that had eluded even the legendary marathon swimmer, Diana Nyad, met with a crushing defeat. The relentless currents, the stinging jellyfish, the exhaustion that threatened to consume her, all conspired to thwart her dream. But instead of succumbing to defeat, Nyad embraced the lessons learned, the insights gained from her first encounter with the formidable Straits. She analyzed every detail, scrutinized every aspect of her previous attempt, her resolve hardened by the sting of failure.

The years that followed were a testament to her unyielding determination. She meticulously planned, trained relentlessly, and studied the unpredictable currents with the fervor of a scientist. She pushed her physical limits, refining her swimming technique, adapting to the unforgiving ocean conditions. Her determination, fueled by a deep-seated belief that she could achieve what others deemed impossible, became her guiding star.

In her second attempt, Nyad faced a formidable opponent - the relentless sting of box jellyfish. The pain was excruciating, the threat of severe allergic reactions, a constant specter. Yet, Nyad persisted. She wore a full-body suit designed to shield her from the venomous creatures, a testament to her unwavering determination to push through the physical pain and emotional toll. Despite the discomfort, the fear, and the threat of the jellyfish, Nyad refused to yield.

Driven by an indomitable spirit, Nyad eventually achieved her goal. Her triumph was not merely a personal victory, it was a resounding affirmation of the power of human resilience. It was a story that resonated with audiences across the globe, a testament to the human capacity to overcome seemingly insurmountable challenges. Nyad's determination became a beacon of hope, an inspiration to those who dared to dream, who believed that no obstacle was too great, no dream too ambitious.

Nyad's journey transcends the realm of sports; it's a powerful narrative about the human spirit, a testament to the transformative power of determination. It's a story that inspires individuals to face their own challenges with unwavering resolve, to believe in the possibility of achieving the seemingly impossible. Nyad's story, etched in the annals of human achievement, is a timeless narrative that reminds us that our potential is boundless, our limits self-imposed, and our dreams, when fueled by relentless determination, can indeed become reality. .

## *Continued advocacy for ocean conservation*

Diana Nyad's relentless pursuit of the impossible, culminating in her historic swim from Cuba to Florida, transcended the realm of athletic achievement. It served as a platform, a beacon of awareness, for a cause deeply entwined with her spirit: ocean conservation. Nyad's journey, fueled by a deep reverence for the natural world, became a clarion call, urging the world to acknowledge the ocean's vulnerability and the urgent need for its protection. Her story, etched in the annals of human resilience, resonated with an audience far beyond the confines of the swimming world, sparking a global conversation about the critical state of our oceans. .

Beyond the physical feat, Nyad's swim underscored the ocean's precarious state. The once-pristine waters she traversed, teeming with life, were now increasingly threatened by pollution, overfishing, and climate change. Her experience, marked by encounters with plastic debris and the chilling effects of rising ocean temperatures, highlighted the stark reality of the human impact on the marine environment. Nyad's narrative, woven with vivid imagery and powerful emotions, served as a poignant reminder of the interconnectedness of our planet and the urgent need for action.

Nyad's advocacy extended beyond the narrative of her swim. She became a vocal ambassador for ocean conservation, utilizing her newfound platform to educate and inspire. Through public speaking engagements, documentaries, and her bestselling memoir, she shared her experiences, emphasizing the vital role the ocean plays in our ecosystem and the dire consequences of its degradation. Her voice, infused with passion and authority, resonated with audiences, prompting them to reexamine their relationship with the ocean and embrace a sense of responsibility for its preservation.

Her advocacy was not limited to raising awareness. Nyad actively engaged in concrete efforts to protect the ocean. She partnered with organizations dedicated to marine conservation, lending her name and influence to their initiatives. She supported research projects aimed at understanding the impact of climate change on marine life and advocated for policies promoting sustainable fishing practices. Her unwavering commitment to ocean conservation transcended the realm of rhetoric, translating into tangible action.

Nyad's relentless pursuit of the impossible extended beyond the physical realm. It encompassed a commitment to safeguarding the very foundation of life on Earth - the ocean. Her story, an epic tale of human endurance and perseverance, became a powerful testament to the strength of human spirit and the urgency of environmental action. Through her continued advocacy, Nyad inspired a generation of ocean enthusiasts and instilled in them a profound sense of responsibility for the future of our planet. .

Her impact resonated far beyond the confines of the swimming community, igniting a global conversation about the health of our oceans. Nyad's journey, both physically and metaphorically, illuminated the vital role of the ocean in sustaining life and the urgent need to protect it for generations to come. The legacy of her swim extends beyond the realm of athletic achievement, serving as a potent symbol of human resilience and a beacon of hope for the future of our planet. It is a testament to the power of individual action and the enduring spirit of conservation that Nyad embodied, forever linking her name with the fight for the health of our oceans. .

.

# Chapter 8: Beyond the Swim

## Writing, speaking, and sharing her story

Diana Nyad's "Find a Way" philosophy, born from her relentless pursuit of the impossible, resonates deeply within the narrative of "The Pursuit of the Impossible." Chapter 8, aptly titled "Beyond the Swim," serves as a testament to this ethos, showcasing Nyad's unwavering dedication to sharing her story and inspiring others to confront their own challenges.

The chapter opens with Nyad's post-swim experience, a whirlwind of media attention and public adulation. While acknowledging the significance of her accomplishment, Nyad navigates this newfound fame with a quiet grace, emphasizing the journey's emotional and psychological impact over the tangible achievement. She reflects on the profound loneliness of the swim, the existential moments of doubt, and the unwavering spirit that propelled her forward. This raw vulnerability, devoid of self-aggrandizement, further amplifies her message: a testament to the power of human resilience in the face of seemingly insurmountable odds.

Nyad's narrative transcends the realm of athletic achievement, delving into the universal human experience of confronting adversity. She skillfully weaves together anecdotes of her childhood, the tragic loss of her father, and the personal struggles she faced throughout her career, highlighting the profound impact these experiences had on her mental fortitude. These personal reflections serve as relatable touchstones, allowing readers to connect with her story on a deeper, emotional level.

Through her captivating storytelling, Nyad seamlessly blends personal anecdotes with practical insights, offering guidance to those who seek to overcome their own challenges. She delves into the importance of cultivating a growth mindset, the role of visualization in achieving seemingly impossible goals, and the power of surrounding oneself with a strong support network. These practical takeaways elevate her narrative from a mere account of a remarkable feat to a guidebook for personal transformation.

"Beyond the Swim" extends beyond the confines of the book, illustrating Nyad's unwavering commitment to sharing her story with the world. Her public speaking engagements, filled with captivating anecdotes and inspirational messages, serve as a powerful platform for reaching diverse audiences. Her TED Talks, in particular, have garnered millions of views, showcasing her ability to communicate her message in a clear, concise, and impactful manner. This unwavering dedication to sharing her story serves as a powerful testament to the transformative power of the human spirit.

Nyad's writing style is characterized by its honesty, vulnerability, and unwavering optimism. Her prose is clear, concise, and engaging, drawing readers into the heart of her experience. She avoids jargon and technical language, ensuring that her message is accessible to a wide audience. This accessibility, coupled with her genuine desire to inspire and empower, has solidified her position as a modern-day role model.

"The Pursuit of the Impossible" is more than just an account of a remarkable athletic feat. It is a testament to the resilience of the human spirit, a guide for navigating the challenges of life, and a powerful reminder that we are all capable of achieving the seemingly impossible. Nyad's dedication to sharing her story, both through writing and public speaking, is a powerful example of the transformative power of storytelling. She skillfully blends her personal journey with practical advice, offering readers a roadmap for navigating their own challenges and realizing their own potential. .

## *Establishing a foundation for water sports and youth development*

Diana Nyad's "The Pursuit of the Impossible" transcends a mere chronicle of a remarkable athletic feat; it embodies a powerful testament to the human spirit's ability to overcome seemingly insurmountable challenges. Beyond the captivating narrative of her historic swim from Cuba to Florida, the book unveils a profound message about the crucial role of water sports in fostering resilience, discipline, and personal growth, particularly within the realm of youth development. Nyad's journey, meticulously recounted in the book, serves as a powerful catalyst, inspiring readers to embrace the transformative power of water sports.

The book's profound impact extends beyond the realm of athletic achievement, delving into the transformative power of water sports in shaping character and building essential life skills. Nyad's relentless pursuit of her goal, characterized by unwavering determination and meticulous planning, embodies the fundamental tenets of water sports. The very nature of swimming, with its inherent challenges of physical exertion, mental fortitude, and unwavering focus, mirrors the demanding yet rewarding process of personal development. .

Nyad's story resonates deeply with youth development programs focused on cultivating resilience, discipline, and a sense of personal accomplishment. Her unwavering determination, meticulously outlined in the book, becomes a beacon of inspiration, demonstrating the transformative power of perseverance. The book emphasizes the importance of goal setting, a core principle of successful water sports programs. Nyad's meticulous planning, her systematic approach to training, and her unwavering focus on achieving her objective, serve as tangible examples for young athletes. They learn to set ambitious goals, break them down into smaller, attainable steps, and approach their endeavors with a disciplined and focused mindset.

"The Pursuit of the Impossible" doesn't merely celebrate Nyad's triumph; it delves into the crucial role of mentors and support systems in nurturing young athletes. Nyad's narrative, interwoven with anecdotes of her early days in the pool, highlights the profound impact of positive role models and supportive environments. She underscores the vital role of coaches, mentors, and communities in fostering a passion for water sports and providing the necessary guidance for aspiring young athletes. Her story underscores the need for structured programs, accessible facilities, and knowledgeable mentors to nurture and guide aspiring young water athletes. .

Moreover, the book delves into the profound impact of water sports on building confidence and self-esteem, crucial aspects of personal growth and development. Nyad's narrative, infused with her experiences as a young swimmer, illuminates the transformative power of water sports in fostering a sense of accomplishment and self-belief. The book emphasizes the inherent sense of self-reliance and discipline that swimming and other water sports cultivate, fostering a sense of mastery over one's environment and a growing belief in personal capabilities. This reinforces the critical role of water sports in boosting confidence, a vital attribute for young people navigating the complexities of adolescence and young adulthood. .

"The Pursuit of the Impossible" transcends a biographical tale; it serves as a powerful advocate for the inclusion and accessibility of water sports, especially for underprivileged youth. Nyad's journey underscores the transformative power of water sports in promoting physical health, mental well-being, and personal growth, irrespective of socioeconomic background. Her story, brimming with resilience and determination, becomes a powerful inspiration for young people facing adversity. It emphasizes the need for programs that break down barriers to participation, ensuring that all youth, regardless of their circumstances, have access to the benefits of water sports.

Furthermore, Nyad's narrative highlights the broader cultural and social impact of water sports, fostering a sense of community and shared purpose. Her journey, documented in the book, underscores the importance of collective support and collaboration, emphasizing the power of shared dreams and collective efforts. It highlights the crucial role of water sports in building strong bonds, fostering camaraderie, and promoting a sense of belonging, particularly within communities where access to these activities is limited.

Nyad's book serves as a powerful advocate for the inclusion and accessibility of water sports, especially for underprivileged youth. It underscores the transformative power of water sports in promoting physical health, mental well-being, and personal growth, irrespective of socioeconomic background. Her journey, brimming with resilience and determination, becomes a powerful inspiration for young people facing adversity. It emphasizes the need for programs that break down barriers to participation, ensuring that all youth, regardless of their circumstances, have access to the benefits of water sports. .

The book serves as a powerful testament to the enduring legacy of Diana Nyad, one that extends far beyond the realm of athletic achievement. Nyad's story, as documented in "The Pursuit of the Impossible," serves as a potent reminder of the transformative power of water sports, not just as a physical activity, but as a vital force in fostering personal growth, resilience, and a sense of community. It inspires individuals, especially young people, to embrace the challenges inherent in water sports, recognizing their capacity for personal transformation and the potential to achieve the seemingly impossible. Nyad's legacy, firmly anchored in the pages of her book, serves as a powerful advocate for the vital role of water sports in shaping the lives of countless young people, empowering them to pursue their dreams, overcome adversity, and ultimately, achieve their own pursuit of the impossible.

## Continuing to pursue challenges

Diana Nyad's life, as chronicled in "Find a Way," is not merely a testament to athletic prowess, but a compelling narrative of unyielding determination, resilience, and the pursuit of seemingly impossible dreams. Nyad's journey is not defined by her triumphs alone, but by her unwavering spirit in the face of countless setbacks and failures. Her story is one of perpetual self-challenge, constantly pushing the boundaries of what she believed was possible, both physically and mentally.

Nyad's early years, marked by a childhood spent in the water and a natural affinity for swimming, laid the foundation for her future endeavors. However, her ambitions extended beyond the mere act of swimming. She yearned to conquer challenges, to test the limits of human endurance, and to prove that seemingly impossible feats could be achieved with unwavering dedication and a fierce will to succeed. This desire was ingrained in her, fueled by an inherent sense of adventure and a thirst for the unknown.

After retiring from competitive swimming, Nyad embarked on a series of challenges that reflected her unwavering pursuit of pushing boundaries. She transitioned from the world of competitive sports to the realm of endurance swimming, initially aiming for a record-breaking swim across the English Channel. This pursuit, while seemingly daunting to many, was merely the first step in a journey of audacious undertakings. The English Channel swim, though successful, was merely a stepping stone, a prelude to a series of even more ambitious endeavors.

Nyad's ambition grew, culminating in her ultimate goal: a solo swim across the Florida Straits, a 110-mile stretch of open water separating Cuba from Florida. This was no mere athletic endeavor; it was a test of human resilience, a battle against the elements, and a confrontation with the very essence of what it meant to push oneself beyond perceived limitations.

This journey, however, was not a straight path to success. Multiple attempts, fraught with challenges and setbacks, marred Nyad's pursuit. She faced fierce currents, unpredictable weather, and a relentless barrage of jellyfish stings. Yet, she refused to surrender. Each failed attempt fueled her determination, each setback reinforcing her unwavering resolve.

The sheer magnitude of the challenge, coupled with the relentless physical and mental strain, would have deterred many. Yet, Nyad's spirit remained unyielding. She continued to train, meticulously studying the currents, honing her swimming technique, and preparing both physically and mentally for the grueling task ahead. Her commitment to the pursuit, her unwavering belief in her own ability to succeed, and her refusal to succumb to self-doubt formed the cornerstone of her extraordinary journey.

In the end, after four failed attempts and years of preparation, Nyad finally conquered the Florida Straits. Her triumph was not simply about achieving a physical feat, but about proving the power of human spirit, the indomitable will to overcome seemingly insurmountable obstacles. It was a testament to the fact that even in the face of adversity, with unwavering determination, even the seemingly impossible can be achieved.

Nyad's story, however, transcends the realm of sports and athletics. It speaks to the core of the human spirit, the innate desire to push boundaries, to confront challenges, and to strive for excellence. Her journey is a reminder that even in the face of overwhelming obstacles, with unwavering determination and a belief in oneself, even the most daunting challenges can be overcome. It is a testament to the enduring power of the human spirit, an inspiration for us all to embrace challenges, to never give up on our dreams, and to strive for greatness in all that we do.

Nyad's legacy extends beyond her athletic accomplishments. It is her unwavering spirit, her relentless pursuit of challenging goals, and her unwavering belief in the power of the human spirit that inspire generations to come. Her story reminds us that limitations are self-imposed, that the seemingly impossible can be achieved with unwavering determination, and that the pursuit of challenging goals, regardless of the outcome, is a journey worth taking. .

# Chapter 9: Facing Challenges

## Overcoming setbacks and obstacles

Diana Nyad's pursuit of swimming from Cuba to Florida, chronicled in her book "The Pursuit of the Impossible," is a testament to the indomitable human spirit, showcasing the transformative power of resilience in the face of adversity. Her journey, marked by numerous setbacks and obstacles, is not merely a tale of athletic prowess but a profound reflection on the human capacity for perseverance and the enduring impact of setbacks on shaping character.

Nyad's first attempt in 1978, undertaken with the confidence of youth and athleticism, ended abruptly due to a relentless current and a subsequent encounter with a jellyfish swarm, a potent reminder that nature's forces could be overwhelming. This initial failure, while disheartening, sowed the seeds of a deep determination within Nyad. It ignited a yearning to conquer not just the physical distance but also the fear and doubt that had crept into her mind.

The decades that followed saw Nyad grappling with the relentless pull of life's demands. She found solace and purpose in journalism, writing, and public speaking, yet the allure of the Cuba-Florida swim lingered. The physical and mental scars of her first attempt, however, left a profound impact, creating an internal conflict that was not easily resolved. This period highlights the complex interplay between ambition and fear, where the pursuit of one's dreams can be intertwined with the weight of past failures.

In 2005, at the age of 58, Nyad decided to attempt the swim once more, spurred by a renewed sense of purpose and an understanding that age should not be a barrier to achieving one's aspirations. This attempt, however, was cut short due to severe weather, a constant reminder of the formidable forces of nature. Yet, Nyad refused to be defeated. This setback, rather than extinguishing her flame, only fueled her determination to push her limits even further. .

It was the 2011 attempt that truly tested Nyad's spirit. The relentless onslaught of jellyfish stings, the grueling physical demands, and the psychological fatigue took their toll. Nyad's body bore the weight of her effort, her skin blistered and her limbs trembling. Yet, her resolve remained unshaken. She persevered, fueled by an unwavering belief in her own capabilities. The pain and exhaustion, however, were not her sole adversary. The ever-present threat of a shark attack, a haunting reminder of the dangers lurking beneath the ocean's surface, added a layer of fear and uncertainty to her journey. The threat of encountering these apex predators, combined with the physical exhaustion, pushed Nyad to her absolute limits, testing her mental and emotional strength.

The years that followed saw Nyad working tirelessly to improve her technique and find ways to overcome the challenges she had faced. She embraced new technologies, focusing on the development of a specially designed protective suit to mitigate the effects of jellyfish stings. This relentless pursuit of innovation, driven by a combination of scientific rigor and personal determination, exemplified Nyad's unwavering commitment to conquering the seemingly insurmountable.

Finally, in 2013, at the age of 64, Nyad achieved her dream. She swam from Cuba to Florida, conquering the distance and shattering the world record for the longest ocean swim without a cage. This victory, however, was not merely a triumph of athleticism. It was a testament to the power of resilience, a demonstration that setbacks can be transformed into stepping stones to ultimate achievement.

Nyad's journey serves as a profound reminder that overcoming obstacles requires a deep commitment to personal growth. Her experience highlights the transformative power of setbacks in shaping character, pushing individuals to find reserves of strength they never knew they possessed. It is not the absence of setbacks but rather the ability to learn from them, adapt, and persevere that defines our capacity for success. . .

Her unwavering determination, combined with her willingness to embrace failure as a catalyst for growth, allowed Nyad to redefine the boundaries of human endurance. She defied conventional wisdom, demonstrating that age is not a limitation, but rather a testament to the potential for growth and transformation. Nyad's story is not merely about swimming; it is about the human spirit's relentless pursuit of its dreams, even in the face of adversity. It is a reminder that the journey itself, marked by challenges and setbacks, is often more enriching and transformative than the destination itself. . .

## Dealing with doubt, criticism, and injuries

The ninth chapter of Diana Nyad's "The Pursuit of the Impossible" delves deeply into the relentless assault of doubt, criticism, and injury that relentlessly tested her resolve as she pursued her audacious dream of swimming from Cuba to Florida without a cage. This chapter reveals not only the physical and emotional toll these challenges exacted, but also the indomitable spirit that propelled Nyad forward.

Nyad's journey wasn't just a physical feat; it was a relentless battle against the whispers of doubt that crept into her consciousness. Throughout her training and preparation, the specter of failure loomed large. The grueling swims in shark-infested waters, the relentless training regimen, and the constant threat of injury chipped away at her confidence. The doubts weren't merely external voices; they were internal demons, whispering insidious suggestions that her dream was folly, that she was too old, too vulnerable, and destined to fail.

Beyond the internal struggles, Nyad faced a barrage of criticism from those who deemed her ambition foolhardy. Skeptics dismissed her quest as a publicity stunt, a reckless gamble with her life. Experts predicted her demise, citing the overwhelming odds stacked against her. These voices, amplified by the media, sought to diminish her efforts and paint her as a delusional dreamer chasing an impossible dream. Yet, Nyad remained resolute, using these criticisms as fuel to ignite her determination.

The relentless onslaught of doubt and criticism was further complicated by a persistent wave of injuries that threatened to derail her entire endeavor. Her body, pushed to its limits, responded with aches, pains, and debilitating setbacks. Jellyfish stings, debilitating cramps, and a near-fatal encounter with a storm left her physically battered and emotionally drained. Each setback, each injury, brought with it a renewed wave of doubt, a stark reminder of the daunting task ahead.

The chapter delves into the specific injuries Nyad encountered and the profound impact they had on her mental state. The excruciating pain of jellyfish stings, the crippling cramps that threatened to paralyze her, and the terrifying experience of being caught in a violent storm - each ordeal served as a stark reminder of the fragility of her body and the unforgiving nature of the challenge. The chapter reveals the mental fortitude required to push through such agonizing pain and the determination needed to overcome the overwhelming fear that accompanied each setback.

Through it all, Nyad's resilience emerges as a defining characteristic. She refused to succumb to the negativity, choosing instead to channel her pain into a renewed sense of purpose. Each injury, each setback, became a testament to her unwavering determination. She drew strength from the support of her team, the unwavering belief of her loved ones, and the unwavering faith in her own abilities.

Nyad's journey is not simply a tale of athletic prowess; it is a testament to the human spirit's capacity to overcome insurmountable odds. It is a narrative that transcends the boundaries of physical achievement, delving into the depths of human resilience, the power of unwavering determination, and the unyielding pursuit of a dream against all odds. The chapter reveals that achieving the impossible is not just about physical strength, it's about the indomitable spirit that refuses to be broken by doubt, criticism, or injury.

It is about the unwavering conviction that what seems impossible today can become reality tomorrow, driven by an unyielding commitment to a dream.

## The importance of perseverance and resilience

Diana Nyad's "Find a Way" mantra, the driving force behind her audacious attempt to swim from Cuba to Florida, encapsulates the core of her story: the importance of perseverance and resilience. Her journey, a testament to the human spirit's ability to overcome seemingly insurmountable odds, transcends the realm of mere athletic achievement. It is a poignant exploration of the power of unwavering determination, a commitment to a dream that refuses to be extinguished by failure or adversity. .

Nyad's initial attempt in 1978, cut short by a storm, planted the seed of an ambition that would blossom into a lifelong pursuit. The years that followed, filled with triumphs and setbacks, became a crucible for her spirit. Each failed attempt, each near-death experience, served not as a deterrent, but as fuel for her determination. The stings of defeat, the whispers of doubt, were met with an unwavering conviction to find a way, to conquer the odds.

Her story is not simply one of physical endurance. It is a narrative woven with threads of mental fortitude, emotional strength, and unwavering faith in oneself. Her ability to confront the debilitating effects of jellyfish stings, the constant threat of sharks, and the relentless onslaught of the elements speaks volumes about her unyielding resolve. The physical pain, the mental exhaustion, the gnawing fear, were all but mere obstacles in her path, challenges to be overcome.

Nyad's resilience is not merely a matter of grit; it is an embodiment of the human capacity for adaptation and growth. She recognized that fear is a powerful force, but a force that can be conquered through self-belief and a relentless pursuit of one's dreams. The doubts that plagued her, the voices that whispered failure, became the very motivators that pushed her forward. Each setback, each obstacle, became a stepping stone on her path to triumph..

Her final attempt, at the age of 64, marked the culmination of years of relentless pursuit. It was a testament to her refusal to accept the limitations imposed by age, a challenge to the notion that dreams have an expiration date. The exhaustion, the pain, the fears - all these were mere whispers compared to the resounding echo of her unwavering belief in herself. The swim, a physical feat of extraordinary endurance, was also a triumph of the human spirit, a testament to the indomitable power of perseverance.

Nyad's journey is a reminder that the impossible is not an end, but a starting point. It is a clarion call to confront the limitations we impose on ourselves and to embrace the possibility of achieving what seems unimaginable. Her story resonates because it reflects a universal truth: within each of us lies a wellspring of resilience, an unyielding spirit that can overcome the most formidable obstacles..

Her unwavering determination, her unyielding faith in herself, and her unwavering belief in the possibility of achieving the impossible, are the enduring legacies of her journey. Diana Nyad's story is not just about swimming from Cuba to Florida; it is about the human spirit's capacity for perseverance, resilience, and the unwavering pursuit of one's dreams. It is a story that transcends sport and inspires us all to believe in the power of our own potential, to embrace the challenge, and to find our own "way.".

# Chapter 10: The Power of Belief

## The role of self-confidence and determination

Diana Nyad's "The Pursuit of the Impossible" is a testament not just to physical endurance, but to the indomitable spirit that resides within the human psyche. Her journey, a relentless pursuit of swimming the Florida Straits without a cage, is a narrative woven with threads of unwavering self-confidence and relentless determination. The book is not simply a chronicle of a singular athletic feat, but a profound exploration of the human capacity to conquer seemingly insurmountable obstacles through the sheer force of belief in oneself.

Nyad's self-confidence is not a boastful arrogance, but a quiet, unwavering belief in her own abilities. It stems from a lifetime of dedication to her craft, a meticulous understanding of her physical and mental strengths, and a steadfast refusal to accept limitations imposed by others. In the face of daunting challenges, be it the frigid waters, the relentless currents, or the ever-present threat of jellyfish stings, Nyad's confidence acts as a guiding beacon. It empowers her to face fear head-on, to push past pain, and to embrace the uncertainty that comes with attempting the impossible. She doesn't simply believe she can swim the Straits, she knows she can. This certainty is not a delusion, but a carefully cultivated self-awareness forged through years of training, experience, and self-reflection.

Determination is the engine that propels Nyad's journey. It fuels her tireless training, pushing her to the limits of her physical and mental capacity. It's the force that compels her to persevere through the crushing weight of setbacks, the despair of near-failure, and the gnawing doubts that inevitably arise. Throughout her struggles, Nyad's determination never falters. It manifests in her meticulous preparation, her meticulous planning, and her refusal to surrender to fatigue, fear, or pain. It is this unwavering determination that allows her to overcome the odds, to endure the unimaginable, and ultimately to achieve the seemingly impossible...

"The Pursuit of the Impossible" transcends the boundaries of a typical sports autobiography. It delves into the profound depths of human potential, revealing how self-confidence and determination can act as catalysts for extraordinary achievements. Nyad's journey is a poignant reminder that the human spirit, when armed with belief in oneself and an unwavering resolve, can surmount seemingly insurmountable obstacles and achieve what was once thought impossible.

The book is a masterclass in self-belief, a powerful illustration of the transformative power of unwavering conviction. Nyad's story is not just about a triumphant swim, but about the journey of a human being who dared to dream big, to embrace the unknown, and to defy the limits imposed by fear and doubt. It is a compelling testament to the inherent resilience of the human spirit and the transformative power of self-belief. Through Nyad's journey, we witness the profound truth that when we truly believe in ourselves, the limits of the possible expand beyond our wildest imaginings.

## Visualizing success and overcoming fear

Diana Nyad's "The Pursuit of the Impossible" is a compelling narrative that transcends the realm of mere athletic achievement. It's a deeply personal journey that explores the intricate dance between belief, fear, and the indomitable spirit of a woman who dared to dream beyond the limitations imposed by societal expectations and the whispers of doubt. Nyad's story isn't simply about conquering the physical challenges of swimming the treacherous Straits of Florida, but about conquering the internal struggles of self-belief and fear, the constant, sometimes insidious companions that can hold us back from reaching our full potential.

The book resonates with readers precisely because it delves into the intricacies of the human psyche. Nyad doesn't shy away from exposing her vulnerabilities, her moments of doubt and despair. She vividly recounts her early encounters with fear, the fear of failure that almost deterred her from pursuing her dreams. This early exposure to fear wasn't merely an obstacle she had to overcome, but a constant companion she had to learn to manage, to understand, and to ultimately harness as a motivator.

A significant portion of the book is dedicated to Nyad's personal journey of cultivating a mindset of unwavering belief. This wasn't a sudden epiphany but a conscious, painstaking process that required introspection, mental discipline, and a relentless pursuit of self-discovery. Nyad acknowledges the power of visualization, a technique she employed not just to imagine the physical act of swimming, but to visualize the mental fortitude necessary to navigate the challenges that lay ahead. By vividly picturing her success, by creating a mental blueprint of her journey, she was able to program her mind for resilience, for enduring the physical pain and mental torment that inevitably accompanied such an endeavor.

The power of visualization transcends the realm of athletic pursuits. It's a tool anyone can utilize to overcome fear, to achieve their goals, and to transform their perceived limitations into opportunities for growth. Nyad's narrative serves as a powerful testament to the transformative power of belief. She illustrates how believing in oneself, even when faced with overwhelming odds, can unlock hidden reservoirs of strength and determination. This unwavering belief wasn't merely a mental exercise, it was a fundamental shift in perspective, a conscious choice to focus on the possibilities rather than the limitations.

Nyad's story isn't a linear narrative of success. It's a testament to the human spirit's ability to persevere through setbacks, to rise from defeat with a renewed sense of purpose. Her initial attempts to swim the Florida Straits were met with failure, with the harsh realities of nature and the limitations of her own physical endurance forcing her to concede defeat. Yet, she didn't allow these failures to extinguish her belief. Instead, she analyzed her mistakes, identified areas for improvement, and, most importantly, she refused to let fear paralyze her. This resilience, this unwavering commitment to her dream, is a cornerstone of Nyad's story.

The book delves deep into the emotional toll of fear, exploring how it manifests not just in physical sensations like shortness of breath and trembling limbs, but also in the insidious whispers of self-doubt that erode confidence and threaten to derail even the most determined individual. Nyad doesn't shy away from the psychological battles she fought, the moments when fear threatened to overwhelm her, and the strategies she employed to combat it. She describes the use of visualization, positive affirmations, and the unwavering support of her team as crucial tools in her arsenal.

Ultimately, Nyad's story is about the transformative power of facing one's fears. It's not about eliminating fear, but about recognizing it as a natural human response and learning to navigate its complexities. Nyad's journey is a powerful reminder that fear can be a catalyst for growth, a driving force that compels us to step outside our comfort zones and to push the boundaries of what we believe is possible.

"The Pursuit of the Impossible" isn't simply a story about swimming; it's a profound reflection on the human spirit's capacity for resilience, determination, and the transformative power of belief. Nyad's story resonates with readers because it captures the universal struggles we all face - the fear of failure, the doubts that plague us, and the longing to achieve something extraordinary. Her journey serves as an inspiration, a testament to the fact that even the most ambitious dreams can be realized with unwavering belief, a strategic approach to conquering fear, and a relentless pursuit of one's potential.

## Inspiring others to achieve their own goals

Diana Nyad's "The Pursuit of the Impossible" stands as a testament to the power of belief. The book, an account of her extraordinary journey to swim from Cuba to Florida, transcends the realm of mere sports autobiography, becoming a powerful manifesto for personal growth and the pursuit of seemingly insurmountable goals. Nyad's story, interwoven with personal reflections, philosophical musings, and poignant anecdotes, becomes a powerful catalyst for inspiring others to push their own boundaries, igniting within them a belief in their own capabilities.

Nyad's journey, fraught with physical and mental challenges, reveals the inherent strength of the human spirit. Facing relentless currents, jellyfish stings, and the ever-present threat of sharks, Nyad endured physical pain and exhaustion beyond most people's comprehension. Yet, she persevered, fueled by an unwavering belief in her own abilities, a belief that transcended the limitations imposed by societal expectations and physical constraints. Her story underscores the importance of embracing audacious dreams, even those seemingly impossible, and challenging oneself to reach beyond perceived limitations.

Nyad's journey is not merely a testament to physical endurance, but also a testament to the transformative power of mental resilience. She delved into the psychological underpinnings of her quest, exploring the intricate interplay between physical and mental strength. Recognizing that the mind often sets the boundaries of what we believe possible, she cultivated a relentless focus on the desired outcome, a mental fortitude that allowed her to overcome moments of doubt and despair. Through her experience, Nyad illuminates the crucial role that self-belief plays in overcoming obstacles and achieving the seemingly impossible.

Beyond the physical and mental aspects of her journey, Nyad's story resonates deeply on an emotional level. The book delves into her personal history, weaving in tales of familial bonds, childhood dreams, and the profound impact of mentors and loved ones. These personal narratives, interwoven with the narrative of her physical journey, serve to humanize Nyad's quest, revealing the emotional underpinnings of her pursuit. Her story becomes relatable, allowing readers to connect with her on a personal level, recognizing the shared human experience of striving for dreams, facing fears, and ultimately, finding the strength within to overcome seemingly insurmountable challenges.

Nyad's "The Pursuit of the Impossible" offers a valuable lesson in the power of belief. The book delves into the transformative power of belief in *oneself, not just as a tool for achieving goals, but as a fundamental component of human potential. By sharing her story with unflinching honesty and raw vulnerability, Nyad empowers readers to embrace their own dreams, pushing them to believe in their capacity to achieve the seemingly impossible. The book, a compelling narrative of personal growth and human resilience, transcends the confines of the swimming pool, becoming a powerful testament to the enduring power of belief. It inspires readers to look beyond their perceived limitations, to tap into the untapped potential within themselves, and to embark on their own journeys of self-discovery and achievement. .*

.

# Chapter 11: The Transformative Journey

## The transformative nature of endurance swimming

Diana Nyad's "The Pursuit of the Impossible" offers a captivating account of her relentless pursuit to swim the Florida Straits, a feat that had eluded her for decades. However, beyond the physical triumph, her journey serves as a potent testament to the profound transformative power of endurance swimming. It's a journey that transcends the physical limitations of the body, delving into the depths of the human spirit, revealing its inherent capacity for resilience, self-discovery, and profound personal growth.

Nyad's book unveils the transformative nature of endurance swimming through a series of interconnected layers. Firstly, it challenges the inherent limitations we place upon ourselves. As she recounts her initial attempts to conquer the Straits, she narrates the crushing weight of self-doubt, the constant nagging fear of failure, and the deeply ingrained belief that the journey was simply beyond her reach. Yet, with each failed attempt, a fundamental shift begins to take place. Nyad's unwavering commitment to her dream, coupled with a steadfast refusal to accept defeat, gradually dismantle these self-imposed barriers. The act of pushing her physical and mental boundaries, of enduring pain and exhaustion, exposes the arbitrary nature of these self-constructed limitations, unveiling a hidden reservoir of strength and determination that she never knew existed.

The transformative nature of endurance swimming extends beyond the realm of self-discovery to encompass a profound sense of connection with the natural world. Nyad's descriptions of the Straits are not mere geographical observations but rather, deeply personal reflections, imbued with a profound sense of awe and reverence. The vastness of the ocean becomes a canvas for her emotional and spiritual journey, mirroring the vastness of her own internal landscape. This connection transcends the physical act of swimming, becoming a conduit for a deeper understanding of the interconnectedness of all life. The ocean, a force of nature that can be both gentle and unforgiving, compels Nyad to confront her fears, to surrender to the power of the natural world, and to find solace and strength within its embrace.

Furthermore, the transformative journey Nyad recounts goes beyond the individual, highlighting the profound impact endurance swimming can have on communities and relationships. Her quest to conquer the Straits, while deeply personal, becomes a catalyst for collective hope and inspiration. The unwavering support she receives from her team, her family, and the countless individuals who follow her journey, serves as a testament to the power of shared dreams and the strength that can be derived from collective support. This collective engagement, fueled by Nyad's unwavering spirit, transforms her journey into a story of shared triumph, one that transcends individual accomplishments, reminding us of the profound interconnectedness of human experience.

Endurance swimming, as Nyad's journey reveals, becomes an act of radical self-discovery. The physical demands of the sport push individuals beyond their comfort zones, forcing them to confront their deepest fears, their self-limiting beliefs, and their capacity for resilience. The journey, however, goes beyond the physical realm, extending into the depths of the human psyche, fostering a profound sense of connection with the natural world, and igniting a shared sense of purpose and inspiration. This transformative nature of endurance swimming, as depicted in Nyad's "The Pursuit of the Impossible", becomes a testament to the boundless capacity of the human spirit, reminding us that even the most impossible dreams can be realized through unwavering determination and the unwavering pursuit of personal growth.

Beyond the mere act of swimming, Nyad's journey becomes a profound exploration of the human condition. The physical challenge serves as a metaphor for the challenges we all face in life, the obstacles we encounter on our paths toward self-realization and our dreams. Her story becomes a blueprint for overcoming adversity, a testament to the power of perseverance, and a reminder that we are all capable of achieving the impossible when we believe in ourselves and our potential. .

Nyad's book is not simply a story of athletic achievement; it is a poignant exploration of the transformative power of endurance swimming, a journey that delves into the depths of human potential, revealing the profound interconnectedness between physical endurance, mental strength, and the spirit's boundless capacity for self-discovery. The journey she recounts is not only about reaching a specific destination but also about the transformative process of embracing the journey itself, a process that reshapes not only the individual but also the communities that share in the experience. It is a journey that reminds us that the pursuit of the impossible is not about the destination but the transformative power of the journey itself.

## How swimming has shaped her life and perspective

Diana Nyad's relationship with swimming transcends a mere sport. It's a profound and transformative force that has shaped her life, her perspective, and her very identity. From her earliest childhood experiences in the water to her legendary feats of endurance, swimming has been a constant companion, a source of both joy and challenge, pushing her to her limits and beyond.

Nyad's initial encounters with the ocean were deeply formative. Growing up in Florida, she was surrounded by the vibrant waters of the Gulf Stream, a landscape that instilled in her a sense of awe and wonder. The ocean was more than just a body of water; it was a living, breathing entity, a source of inspiration and a constant reminder of the boundless possibilities that life held. As a young girl, Nyad discovered the liberating freedom that swimming offered, the feeling of weightlessness and the sense of boundless energy that came with propelling herself through the water. It was a feeling that she would cherish for the rest of her life.

Swimming became more than just a recreational activity for Nyad. It became a way of life, a philosophy that permeated her thoughts and actions. It taught her the importance of perseverance, the power of setting goals, and the unwavering belief in one's ability to achieve them. In the water, she learned to overcome fear, to push past the limits of her physical and mental endurance, and to find strength within herself that she didn't know existed. These lessons extended far beyond the pool, influencing her approach to life's challenges.

Nyad's athletic career was a testament to the transformative power of swimming. Her early successes in synchronized swimming were merely the beginning of a journey that would take her to the pinnacle of her sport. She excelled in open water swimming, pushing her boundaries and breaking records, proving herself a force to be reckoned with. Her victories were not just about physical prowess; they were about mental strength, determination, and a deep-seated belief in her own potential. .

However, it was Nyad's pursuit of the seemingly impossible that truly defined her relationship with swimming. Her audacious dream of swimming from Cuba to Florida, a feat that had eluded even the most seasoned athletes, became a defining moment in her life. This journey was not just about physical endurance; it was a test of her mental fortitude, her will to persevere, and her ability to push past the limits of human potential. It was a testament to the transformative power of swimming, its ability to ignite a fire within, to inspire resilience, and to show us what we are truly capable of.

Nyad's unwavering commitment to her dream, despite countless setbacks and the naysayers who doubted her ability, was a testament to the lessons she had learned from swimming. It was a journey that pushed her to her absolute limits, forcing her to confront her deepest fears and insecurities. It was a journey that taught her the importance of embracing challenge, of never giving up, and of finding strength in adversity.

The accomplishment of swimming from Cuba to Florida was not just a personal triumph; it was a symbol of hope, inspiration, and the enduring power of the human spirit. It was a testament to the transformative nature of swimming, its ability to empower, to embolden, and to inspire us to reach for our dreams, no matter how impossible they may seem. It was a victory that resonated far beyond the world of sports, inspiring countless others to push past their limitations and to embrace the transformative power of their own inner strength.

Nyad's life is a testament to the transformative power of swimming. It has shaped her perspective, her values, and her very identity. Through its challenges and triumphs, swimming has taught her the importance of perseverance, the power of setting goals, and the unwavering belief in one's own potential. It has taught her the value of embracing challenge, of finding strength in adversity, and of never giving up on her dreams. Nyad's relationship with swimming is not just a personal story; it's a universal tale of the human spirit, its resilience, its tenacity, and its boundless potential. It's a reminder that we are all capable of achieving the seemingly impossible, if we have the courage to dream, the determination to persevere, and the unwavering belief in ourselves. .

## The importance of finding meaning and purpose

Diana Nyad's "The Pursuit of the Impossible" is a testament to the human spirit's enduring ability to conquer seemingly insurmountable challenges, but it also delves deeper, exploring the profound importance of finding meaning and purpose in a life that is often driven by external pressures and fleeting pursuits. Nyad's journey, a relentless pursuit of swimming from Cuba to Florida without a cage, is not merely a story of physical endurance and athletic prowess, but a profound reflection on the search for inner fulfillment and the discovery of a life's purpose that transcends the mundane. .

In the book, Nyad's relentless pursuit of this seemingly impossible feat is fueled by a yearning for something more than mere accomplishment. She acknowledges that the swim is a microcosm of a larger quest, a quest for meaning in a world often characterized by fleeting distractions and superficial pursuits. She writes, "I wanted to find out if I could still feel the fire of my youth, the passion that had once driven me. I wanted to know if I could still push myself to the absolute limit." This desire to reconnect with her inner fire, a fire that had been dormant for years, speaks to a universal human need to find purpose and meaning in life. .

Nyad's unwavering commitment to the swim is not simply about conquering a physical challenge, but about transcending the limitations of self-doubt and societal expectations. She writes, "For years, I had been living a life that felt empty, a life defined by other people's expectations. I was a successful journalist, a respected author, but I felt like I was living a lie. I was not being true to myself." This realization underscores the importance of aligning our actions with our deepest values and aspirations. Nyad's pursuit of this seemingly impossible feat becomes a symbol of reclaiming her own narrative, breaking free from societal norms and pursuing a life that resonates with her authentic self.

Nyad's journey is marked by setbacks and challenges that would have easily deterred anyone else. She endured jellyfish stings, relentless currents, and the constant threat of fatigue and exhaustion. Yet, she persevered, driven by a deep-seated belief in her own potential and a desire to prove that anything is possible if one sets their mind to it. She writes, "I knew that I was capable of so much more than I had ever thought possible. I had always been afraid of failure, but I had learned that failure was just a part of the process." This realization is crucial for understanding the importance of finding meaning and purpose. It is not about achieving perfection or avoiding failure, but about embracing the challenges and setbacks that inevitably come with the pursuit of something greater than oneself.

Beyond the physical endurance and resilience, Nyad's swim becomes a metaphor for the transformative journey of self-discovery. It is a journey that transcends the physical realm, delving into the depths of human consciousness and the power of the human spirit. The journey is not about reaching the finish line, but about the continuous process of self-discovery, the constant striving for growth and transformation. The swim is a symbol of breaking free from the limitations of our own minds, proving that even the most daunting challenges can be overcome with unwavering determination and a clear sense of purpose.

Nyad's relentless pursuit of her goal, a seemingly impossible swim across treacherous waters, reflects a deeper desire to reconnect with her authentic self, to transcend societal expectations, and to prove that the human spirit is capable of extraordinary feats. Her journey serves as a powerful reminder that finding purpose and meaning in life is not about achieving external validation or reaching a predetermined destination, but about embracing the challenges, setbacks, and triumphs that come with the continuous process of self-discovery. .

.

## Chapter 12: Training and Technique

### Details of her training regimen and swimming technique

Diana Nyad's journey to conquer the treacherous waters of the Florida Straits, a seemingly insurmountable feat, was a testament to the indomitable spirit that propelled her to push the limits of human endurance. It was a journey not just across the ocean, but through a rigorous tapestry of training and meticulous refinement of swimming technique. Nyad's unwavering commitment to these two pillars, woven together with an acute understanding of her own physiology and mental fortitude, transformed her into a formidable athlete, capable of conquering a seemingly impossible challenge. .

Training for a swim of such magnitude demanded a comprehensive approach, blending physical prowess with mental resilience. Nyad meticulously crafted a regimented training plan, meticulously honed to address the unique demands of her ambitious undertaking. This plan wasn't merely about churning out miles in the pool; it was about building an arsenal of skills and capabilities that could withstand the relentless assault of the ocean. .

Her training wasn't confined to the water; she understood the vital role of building a robust foundation that extended beyond the pool's edge. Nyad's regimen incorporated rigorous cross-training, incorporating a medley of exercises that targeted various muscle groups. These exercises, including cycling, running, and strength training, served a multifold purpose. They fortified her cardiovascular system, enhanced her core strength, and instilled a level of resilience that would prove essential during her marathon swim.

Beyond the physical, Nyad understood the profound impact of mental fortitude on her journey. She dedicated herself to a rigorous mental training regimen, employing various techniques to cultivate an unwavering mental resolve. She trained her mind to withstand the relentless assault of self-doubt and to harness the power of positive visualization, picturing herself conquering the daunting distance, inch by inch. This mental preparation, coupled with her physical training, created a formidable combination that allowed her to confront the challenge with unwavering resolve.

Nyad's mastery of swimming technique was a crucial component of her success. Her stroke, honed through years of dedicated practice, was a symphony of efficiency and power. Her freestyle stroke, her primary weapon in the water, was characterized by a smooth, rhythmic motion, minimizing energy expenditure while maximizing propulsion. The precision of her movements was a testament to her years of meticulous refinement, where every detail, from the positioning of her hand to the angle of her body, was meticulously honed to achieve optimal efficiency.

The ocean, a formidable adversary, presented unique challenges that required specific adaptations in Nyad's swimming technique. She developed a unique approach to combat the relentless waves, mastering a technique to ride their crests, harnessing their energy for forward momentum. This nuanced adaptation allowed her to navigate the turbulent seas with relative ease, conserving energy and maintaining a consistent pace.

Furthermore, Nyad understood the vital role of nutrition in sustaining her endurance throughout the grueling swim. She meticulously crafted a diet that provided her body with the necessary fuel to power her journey. Her diet was a symphony of balance, incorporating complex carbohydrates for sustained energy, lean protein for muscle recovery, and healthy fats for essential nutrients. She meticulously planned her caloric intake, ensuring she had adequate fuel to sustain her relentless effort without compromising her body's performance.

Nyad's training regimen and swimming technique weren't merely a collection of exercises and movements; they were an intricate dance of physical and mental preparation, meticulously orchestrated to ensure her success. Her dedication to this holistic approach, her unwavering commitment to refining her technique, and her meticulous attention to every detail transformed her from a determined swimmer into a formidable athlete, capable of conquering the seemingly impossible. Her journey was a testament to the power of dedication, perseverance, and an unyielding belief in the human potential to push the boundaries of what's possible.

## The role of nutrition, hydration, and sleep

Diana Nyad's relentless pursuit of swimming the Florida Straits, documented in "The Pursuit of the Impossible," stands as a testament to human endurance. Her journey, however, was not simply a feat of physical strength; it was intricately interwoven with a meticulous approach to nutrition, hydration, and sleep. These seemingly mundane aspects played a pivotal role in Nyad's ability to withstand the grueling physical demands of the swim.

Nyad's understanding of the importance of nutrition during a long-distance swim was evident in her meticulously planned diet. The core of her nutrition strategy revolved around consuming high-calorie, easily digestible foods that provided her body with sustained energy. This involved a steady intake of carbohydrates, essential for fueling muscle activity, along with lean protein, crucial for muscle repair and recovery. To ensure optimal energy levels, she relied heavily on a combination of sports drinks and gels, carefully calculated to maintain a consistent supply of glucose and electrolytes. .

The challenge of maintaining hydration in the harsh ocean environment was a constant concern for Nyad. She faced not only the risk of dehydration from prolonged exposure to the sun and salt water but also the challenge of ingesting enough fluids without compromising her stomach. To address this, Nyad developed a carefully calibrated hydration plan. She strategically consumed water throughout the swim, prioritizing consistent sips rather than large amounts at once, and opting for low-sodium sports drinks to minimize stomach discomfort. .

Beyond the immediate needs of the swim itself, Nyad recognized the crucial role that sleep played in her overall recovery and preparation. The demands of a long-distance swim extend beyond the physical; they also strain the mind, creating a constant need for mental resilience. Nyad's approach to sleep involved a combination of strategies designed to optimize both physical and mental recovery. .

She prioritized sleep hygiene, establishing a consistent sleep schedule and creating a relaxing bedtime routine that allowed her mind and body to unwind after a day of intense physical exertion. This involved minimizing screen time before bed, engaging in calming activities like meditation or reading, and ensuring a comfortable sleep environment. .

Recognizing the importance of recovery, Nyad embraced naps during her training and even incorporated short sleep breaks during the swim itself. These naps, strategically scheduled, provided her with the necessary rest and energy to continue pushing herself to the limit. Nyad's approach to sleep wasn't simply about the quantity of hours but also about the quality of her sleep, ensuring she woke up feeling refreshed and ready to face the next challenge.

Nyad's unwavering focus on nutrition, hydration, and sleep not only fueled her physical performance but also underscored the essential role that these seemingly simple elements play in achieving seemingly impossible goals. By meticulously planning and executing these seemingly mundane aspects of her preparation, Nyad demonstrated that the key to reaching beyond perceived limitations often lies in paying close attention to the foundational elements that support our physical and mental well-being. Her journey, both in the water and in the meticulous attention she paid to these details, serves as a powerful reminder that even the most remarkable achievements are built on a foundation of consistent attention to seemingly mundane aspects of our daily lives. .

## *Strategies for improving speed and endurance*

Diana Nyad's "The Pursuit of the Impossible" is a testament to the human spirit's capacity to conquer seemingly insurmountable challenges. The book chronicles her relentless pursuit of swimming the Florida Straits, a feat previously considered impossible. Nyad's journey, however, goes beyond mere physical endurance; it's a profound exploration of the mind's ability to push beyond perceived limits and discover reservoirs of resilience. Central to this journey is Nyad's dedication to refining her swimming technique and maximizing her physical prowess.

The book delves into the nuances of swimming technique, emphasizing the importance of a streamlined body position. This principle, often referred to as "hydrodynamics," plays a pivotal role in minimizing water resistance and optimizing energy expenditure. Nyad meticulously analyzes the movement of her limbs, striving to maintain a minimal amount of turbulence while maximizing propulsion. This meticulous attention to detail is essential for sustained swimming over long distances, as even slight inefficiencies in technique can lead to exhaustion and hinder progress. .

Beyond technique, the book explores the intricacies of training for endurance events. Nyad's approach is characterized by a methodical and progressive build-up of both swimming volume and intensity. Her training regimen includes long swims in open water, often incorporating challenging currents and environmental conditions. She also utilizes interval training techniques, designed to increase speed and power. By progressively pushing her boundaries, Nyad prepares her body to handle the demands of a marathon swim. .

One crucial aspect of Nyad's training involves mental conditioning. She recognizes the importance of building mental resilience, a critical factor in conquering the psychological challenges of endurance swimming. Nyad employs visualization techniques, focusing on the desired outcome and imagining the physical and emotional sensations associated with success. This mental preparation allows her to stay focused and motivated during the grueling hours of a long swim. .

Central to Nyad's training philosophy is the principle of "mind-body connection. " She emphasizes the interconnectedness of the physical and mental aspects of performance, recognizing that mental strength is crucial for achieving peak physical performance. Nyad's journey highlights the importance of maintaining a positive mindset even in the face of adversity, fostering a belief in one's own ability to overcome challenges. .

Furthermore, Nyad acknowledges the importance of a balanced approach to training. While demanding, her regimen also prioritizes rest and recovery. She emphasizes the need for adequate sleep and proper nutrition, recognizing that these factors are essential for physical and mental rejuvenation. By incorporating these strategies into her training, Nyad ensures that her body is well-equipped to withstand the rigors of prolonged swimming. .

The book goes beyond simply outlining Nyad's training regimen; it offers insights into the psychological factors that contribute to sustained performance. Nyad's story underlines the importance of self-belief, determination, and unwavering focus. It also underscores the crucial role of support systems, with Nyad crediting her team, her coaches, and her loved ones for providing encouragement and guidance throughout her journey. .

Ultimately, Nyad's "The Pursuit of the Impossible" provides a compelling and insightful account of the strategies employed to enhance speed and endurance in swimming. Beyond the specific techniques and training methods, the book delivers a powerful message about the transformative power of perseverance, resilience, and the human spirit's ability to push beyond perceived limitations. Nyad's journey serves as a poignant reminder that with focused training, unwavering determination, and a belief in one's capabilities, even the seemingly impossible can be achieved.

## Chapter 13: Teamwork and Support

### The importance of a supportive team and crew

Diana Nyad's "The Pursuit of the Impossible" is a testament to the power of unwavering determination, fueled by a deeply supportive team and crew. The book, chronicling her decades-long quest to swim from Cuba to Florida without a cage, is a resounding narrative of human resilience, but it's equally a captivating story of how a formidable crew can be the catalyst for achieving the seemingly impossible. Nyad's account vividly illustrates how a supportive network, comprised of individuals with diverse skills and unwavering faith, can provide the essential scaffolding for an ambitious undertaking. . .

It's crucial to recognize that Nyad's journey was not just a physical test, but a psychological one. The vastness of the ocean, the lurking dangers of sharks and jellyfish, and the crushing fatigue tested her resolve at every turn. Here, the strength of her team transcended logistical support, morphing into an invaluable emotional bedrock. The book paints a poignant picture of a team that understood the intricate dance between physical exertion and mental fortitude. They were not just navigators and boat handlers, but also empathetic confidants, understanding that Nyad's success rested on their ability to keep her spirits afloat when the waves of self-doubt crashed down.

The text underscores the significance of a team's ability to adapt and improvise, mirroring the unpredictable nature of the open ocean. Nyad's initial attempts were marred by unforeseen challenges, including a severe jellyfish sting and relentless currents. The crew, instead of succumbing to despair, responded with ingenuity and grit. They meticulously researched the sting's properties, devised protective gear, and adapted their strategies to navigate the shifting tides. This ability to adjust on the fly, demonstrating a deep understanding of both the physical and psychological demands of the endeavor, was paramount to Nyad's ultimate success.

Nyad's account eloquently underscores the importance of a team's cohesiveness, highlighting the powerful synergy that arises when individuals with varied skills and experiences unite under a common goal. The crew consisted of navigators, medics, boat handlers, and even a marine biologist, each with specialized knowledge vital to the mission's success. The book portrays a seamless collaboration, where individual expertise seamlessly blended into a unified force. Each member understood their role within the intricate tapestry of the team, working in concert to navigate the challenges and propel Nyad towards her goal.

The importance of a team's communication is a recurring theme throughout the book. Nyad's narrative vividly portrays the intricate communication network that linked her to her team throughout her swim. From the boat, they conveyed vital information regarding currents, weather conditions, and even potential dangers, allowing Nyad to make informed decisions and navigate the treacherous waters. Equally important was the communication of encouragement and reassurance, a lifeline that kept Nyad's spirit buoyed during moments of doubt and fatigue. This constant flow of information and emotional support served as a vital bridge connecting her to the crew, ensuring her mental and physical wellbeing.

"The Pursuit of the Impossible" goes beyond the thrill of a record-breaking achievement. It's a deep dive into the human spirit, showcasing the crucial role of a cohesive and supportive team in pushing the boundaries of human endurance. Nyad's journey is not merely a testament to her individual determination, but a compelling illustration of how a well-organized and empathetic team can serve as a powerful catalyst for realizing seemingly impossible dreams. The book masterfully illustrates the intricate relationship between individual ambition and the unwavering support of a team, proving that even the most challenging goals can be achieved when the right people come together, united by a shared vision and unwavering belief. .

## *Collaborating with experts and scientists*

Diana Nyad's relentless pursuit of swimming the Florida Straits, a feat considered impossible for decades, wasn't simply a testament to her physical endurance. It was a symphony of collaboration, a collective effort orchestrated by a team of experts and scientists whose contributions were as crucial as Nyad's own. Each member brought unique expertise, forming a tightly interwoven network of knowledge and support that fueled her ambition and, ultimately, enabled her to conquer the seemingly insurmountable. .

Nyad's determination was met with initial skepticism. A history of jellyfish stings, the grueling distance, and the unpredictable currents of the Gulf Stream all presented daunting challenges. It was Dr. Joseph LeDoux, a renowned neuroscientist at New York University, who stepped in to address the mental hurdle. He recognized the importance of Nyad's mindset in navigating the psychological complexities of the attempt. Dr. LeDoux, with his expertise in fear conditioning, helped Nyad develop a strategy to manage anxieties and navigate the mental fatigue that would inevitably arise. .

The threat of marine life, specifically jellyfish, was a significant concern. To tackle this, Nyad collaborated with Dr. Angela Zilka, a renowned marine biologist. Dr. Zilka's deep understanding of jellyfish behavior and ecology proved invaluable. She designed a custom-made "stinger suit" that, while not entirely eliminating stings, offered protection and minimized their severity. Moreover, Dr. Zilka's research provided insight into jellyfish migration patterns, allowing the team to predict and avoid areas of higher concentration, crucial for the success of the attempt. .

The unpredictable currents of the Gulf Stream presented another major obstacle. To overcome this challenge, Nyad sought the expertise of Dr. Brian LaPointe, a renowned oceanographer. Dr. LaPointe, utilizing advanced oceanographic models, developed a complex strategy for navigating the currents. This involved a meticulous analysis of historical data, satellite imagery, and real-time weather forecasts, allowing the team to predict the most favorable currents and minimize Nyad's energy expenditure. .

Nyad's team also included renowned nutritionist, Dr. Tricia Zimmerman, who meticulously tailored a diet plan that would sustain Nyad's energy levels throughout the grueling swim. Dr. Zimmerman's expertise ensured Nyad's nutritional needs were met in a way that would optimize her physical performance and minimize the risk of exhaustion. .

Moreover, Nyad's team included an experienced crew, including a navigator, a boat captain, and a doctor, all trained to provide constant support and monitor Nyad's physical condition. This close-knit team, operating in tandem with the experts mentioned above, played a vital role in ensuring the success of the attempt. They provided Nyad with constant hydration, feeding, and medical attention, allowing her to focus solely on her swim. .

The success of Diana Nyad's historic swim was a testament to the collective power of human collaboration. The expertise of Dr. LeDoux, Dr. Zilka, Dr. LaPointe, Dr. Zimmerman, and the skilled crew combined to overcome seemingly insurmountable obstacles, highlighting the vital role of interdisciplinary collaboration in achieving extraordinary feats. Nyad's journey not only demonstrated the power of human endurance but also highlighted the importance of fostering partnerships between different fields of expertise in pushing the boundaries of human achievement. .

.

## The role of camaraderie and motivation

Diana Nyad's relentless pursuit of swimming the Florida Straits without a cage, as chronicled in her memoir "The Pursuit of the Impossible," is a testament to the transformative power of human connection. Beyond the physical endurance, the book highlights the profound influence of camaraderie and motivation on her journey. Nyad's success wasn't merely an individual triumph, but a collective effort nurtured by the unwavering support of her team.

The book delves into the intricacies of building a team that thrives on mutual trust and understanding. Nyad's crew, a diverse group of professionals, served as much more than just assistants; they were her confidantes, her cheerleaders, and her lifeline. The depth of their commitment transcended their individual roles, becoming a powerful force that propelled her towards the impossible. Nyad's meticulous selection process, valuing experience, resilience, and a shared vision, resulted in a team where each member understood the enormous weight of their collective responsibility. Their shared passion for the challenge, their unwavering belief in Nyad's capabilities, and their willingness to push their own boundaries to support her, fostered a profound sense of unity that transcended individual goals.

The book emphasizes the importance of open communication, acknowledging that a successful team thrives on honest feedback and constructive criticism. Nyad's team embraced vulnerability, allowing each member to express their concerns and share their doubts without fear of judgment. This open dialogue created a space for collective problem-solving, where challenges were addressed collaboratively, reinforcing their shared commitment. They navigated the complexities of human interaction with grace and empathy, understanding that success wasn't just about physical strength, but also about emotional intelligence and resilience.

Nyad's memoir showcases the profound impact of positive reinforcement and motivational strategies. Her crew, acutely aware of the mental and emotional toll of such an ambitious endeavor, employed a diverse range of techniques to keep Nyad's spirits high. They used humor, shared stories of inspiration, and personalized motivational messages to combat the inevitable moments of self-doubt and despair. These strategies, carefully tailored to Nyad's personality and needs, served as a constant reminder of the collective belief in her ability to succeed.

Beyond the technical aspects of swimming, Nyad's success hinges on the unwavering support of her team, whose motivational strategies go beyond mere encouragement. They became her mental compass, guiding her through moments of doubt and fear, reminding her of the unwavering support system she had cultivated. Nyad's story is not solely about overcoming physical limitations, but also about the power of human connection to fuel the pursuit of seemingly impossible goals.

The book also explores the intricate dance between individual motivation and team cohesion. While Nyad's determination and unwavering commitment are undeniable, her success is inextricably linked to the support and encouragement of her crew. Each member contributed to the larger picture, recognizing their individual roles as integral components of the collective effort. They understood that their individual strengths, when combined, would create a force greater than the sum of its parts.

Beyond the technical expertise and physical strength, it was the profound human connection that fueled Nyad's journey. The bond forged between her and her crew transcended mere professional association, transforming into a tapestry of shared experiences, vulnerabilities, and triumphs. Their unwavering faith in each other, their ability to face adversity together, and their unwavering commitment to the common goal of swimming the Florida Straits without a cage are the heart of Nyad's incredible story.

The book's narrative is not simply a celebration of individual achievement, but a testament to the power of human connection, emphasizing that even the most extraordinary feats are achieved through the collective effort of a motivated and united team. Nyad's journey underscores the profound impact of camaraderie and motivation, reminding us that human potential is often unlocked through the unwavering support of those who believe in our dreams. It is a testament to the power of teamwork, reminding us that the pursuit of the impossible becomes attainable when fueled by shared vision, unwavering support, and a profound belief in the strength of human connection. . .

# Chapter 14: The Cuba-Florida Swim: In Depth

## *A detailed account of the planning, preparation, and execution of the swim*

Diana Nyad's epic swim from Cuba to Florida, a journey she meticulously planned and relentlessly prepared for, stands as a testament to human endurance and the unwavering pursuit of an impossible dream. Her 53-hour, 110-mile swim, accomplished in 2013 at the age of 64, was a culmination of years of meticulous planning, rigorous training, and unwavering mental fortitude. Nyad's journey was not merely a physical undertaking; it was a complex endeavor requiring the orchestration of a team, meticulous attention to detail, and an unflinching resolve to overcome the formidable challenges posed by the ocean.

Nyad's planning began long before she set foot in Cuban waters. Recognizing the formidable nature of her undertaking, she assembled a team of experts, each specializing in a crucial aspect of the swim. This team, comprised of experienced oceanographers, navigators, and support crew members, played an instrumental role in her success. Extensive research was conducted to identify the ideal time of year for the swim, considering factors such as water temperature, currents, and potential weather patterns. This meticulous analysis resulted in the selection of September as the target month, a period deemed optimal for favorable conditions.

In preparation for the grueling swim, Nyad embarked on a rigorous training regime designed to push her physical and mental limits. She spent countless hours swimming in open water, simulating the conditions she would encounter in the Florida Straits. These training sessions, often lasting for hours, were designed to build her stamina, endurance, and acclimate her body to the rigors of the journey. Her training was not limited to the pool; Nyad engaged in rigorous strength training and cardiovascular exercises, focusing on building the strength and endurance required to tackle the arduous swim..

In addition to physical training, Nyad recognized the critical role of mental preparedness in her quest. She sought guidance from experienced sports psychologists, who helped her develop strategies for managing the inevitable moments of doubt, fatigue, and fear that would inevitably arise during the swim. She learned techniques for visualizing success, maintaining focus, and channeling her inner strength to overcome adversity. The mental preparation became an integral aspect of her training, ensuring that she was equipped to handle the psychological challenges as formidable as the physical ones.

The execution of Nyad's swim was a meticulously orchestrated undertaking, requiring coordination and precision from every member of her team. The support crew, stationed aboard a specially equipped boat, monitored her progress, communicated instructions, and provided vital support throughout the journey. The crew included expert navigators, experienced medical professionals, and a dedicated team of support personnel, all working in unison to ensure Nyad's safety and well-being..

Nyad's swim, a testament to her unwavering determination, was a grueling test of human endurance. The treacherous currents, unpredictable weather conditions, and the relentless assault of jellyfish posed constant threats to her progress. The relentless cold, a constant companion, gnawed at her body, and exhaustion threatened to overwhelm her. However, through it all, Nyad drew strength from her training, her unwavering mental resolve, and the unwavering support of her team..

The successful completion of her swim marked a historic milestone, not just for Diana Nyad but for the world of open-water swimming. It showcased the power of human resilience, the importance of meticulous planning, and the transformative effect of an unyielding belief in the seemingly impossible. Nyad's extraordinary journey, a testament to the indomitable spirit within, serves as an inspiration for anyone daring to dream big and push the boundaries of what they believe they can achieve.

.

## Facing unpredictable weather, wildlife, and physical limitations

Diana Nyad's journey across the Florida Straits, chronicled in "The Pursuit of the Impossible," was a symphony of human spirit, unwavering determination, and a constant battle against the unforgiving elements. Facing unpredictable weather, hostile marine life, and the relentless wear and tear on her aging body, she pushed herself to the very edge of human endurance, highlighting the remarkable resilience and the profound limitations of the human form.

The unpredictability of the weather loomed large, casting a shadow of uncertainty over every aspect of her journey. The constant threat of storms, often unpredictable and violent, could derail her plans at a moment's notice. Nyad had to navigate treacherous currents, with swirling eddies and riptides threatening to pull her off course. The wind, too, became a formidable opponent, creating mountainous waves that tossed her like a leaf in a hurricane. This constant dance with nature demanded unwavering vigilance, forcing her to adapt to shifting conditions, recalibrate her strategy, and summon the courage to push forward in the face of danger.

The marine life of the Florida Straits posed a constant threat, demanding constant awareness and calculated risk. The shark factor was the most tangible and terrifying, a constant lurking presence in the depths. The possibility of an encounter with a predatory shark, fueled by fear and fueled by the historical reality of previous attempts, hung like a sword of Damocles over her head. Despite the safety measures taken, the fear of a sudden attack, the possibility of a chilling encounter with a creature far more powerful than herself, was a constant companion on her journey. The presence of jellyfish, too, was a source of constant concern. Stinging tentacles, capable of inflicting excruciating pain and potentially delaying her progress or even endangering her life, forced her to constantly assess her environment and maneuver around these gelatinous predators.

Beyond the external threats, Nyad had to confront the internal limitations of her own body. The strain on her muscles, tendons, and ligaments was immense. Days on end of relentless swimming, with no respite, took its toll. Her limbs ached, her body screamed for rest, but she refused to yield. The relentless assault on her physical being, the constant battle against fatigue and pain, tested the very limits of her endurance. She battled with cramps, nausea, and the debilitating effects of exhaustion. Sleep deprivation, a cruel companion on this solitary adventure, sapped her energy and clouded her judgment, adding another layer to the physical and mental challenges she faced.

Nyad's journey was a testament to the power of the human will and the limits of physical endurance. It was a story not only of triumph over formidable obstacles but also a stark reminder of the vulnerability of the human body, its ability to withstand incredible hardship yet ultimately bound by the limits of biology. It was a journey that pushed her to her absolute breaking point, revealing both the remarkable strength and the inevitable fragility of the human spirit. It was a testament to the strength of the human will to push beyond the boundaries of perceived limitations, and a poignant reminder of the humbling reality of human frailty. . .

## The emotional and mental challenges of the journey

Diana Nyad's "The Pursuit of the Impossible" chronicles her relentless pursuit of a seemingly impossible dream: to swim from Cuba to Florida without a cage. Nyad's narrative unveils the intricate dance between physical exhaustion, crippling doubt, and unwavering determination, a dance that ultimately defines the essence of her extraordinary accomplishment.

The initial hours of the swim are characterized by a disconcerting sense of isolation, a stark contrast to the camaraderie of her training sessions. The vastness of the ocean, devoid of landmarks or familiar sights, fosters a sense of disorientation and fear. The vast emptiness of the water mirrors the gnawing uncertainty within Nyad, a fear that her body, honed for years, might not be enough to withstand the relentless currents and the brutal onslaught of jellyfish stings. These physical challenges, coupled with the relentless mental struggle, expose the vulnerability inherent in human endurance.

As the sun dips below the horizon, casting long shadows over the turbulent waters, Nyad finds herself grappling with the ever-present threat of the darkness. The darkness becomes a symbol of the unknowns lurking beneath the surface, both literally and metaphorically. It amplifies her anxieties, conjuring up images of sharks and other unseen dangers. The fear of the unknown, fueled by the crushing loneliness and physical exhaustion, threatens to extinguish the flickering flame of hope within her.

The struggle against the elements becomes a metaphor for her internal struggle. The unforgiving ocean currents, like the relentless doubts that plague her, continuously push against her progress. She must constantly fight against the relentless pull of fear and self-doubt, finding strength in the memory of her long-held dream. The very act of fighting against the relentless currents becomes a symbolic representation of her determination to defy the odds, to push beyond the limitations imposed by her own mind.

Sleep, the only respite from the physical and mental toll, becomes a battleground itself. The constant fear of drifting off and missing crucial navigational signals, the unrelenting pain, and the overwhelming loneliness force her to fight against the allure of unconsciousness. Sleep, a natural human need, becomes a sign of weakness, a concession to fatigue that she must resist. The constant vigilance, the struggle to remain conscious and alert, speaks volumes about the depths of her mental fortitude.

The journey, however, is not solely defined by the struggle. It is also punctuated by moments of profound beauty and awe. Nyad's descriptions of the mesmerizing bioluminescent plankton, the breathtaking sunsets, and the awe-inspiring migration of whales evoke a sense of wonder and a renewed appreciation for the natural world. These moments of beauty serve as reminders of the vastness and wonder of the universe, grounding her in the present and offering a brief reprieve from the torment of doubt.

The companionship of her crew, while not physically present, provides a lifeline of emotional support. Their unwavering belief in her, their constant communication, and their meticulous monitoring of her progress, serve as a source of strength and encouragement. It is their voices, their unwavering faith, that she clings to during her darkest moments, a reminder that she is not alone in her journey.

Through the relentless waves, the relentless doubts, and the relentless pain, Nyad finds her strength in the power of her own mind. The act of swimming is not simply about physical endurance, but about the relentless pursuit of a dream, the unwavering determination to push beyond self-imposed limitations. Each stroke, each moment of pain, each victory over self-doubt, becomes a testament to the extraordinary power of the human spirit, a power that allows us to confront our deepest fears and emerge triumphant. .

## Chapter 15: Environmental Advocacy

### Nyad's passion for ocean conservation

Diana Nyad's journey, a tapestry woven with threads of athletic prowess, unwavering determination, and an unyielding love for the ocean, culminates in a profound commitment to ocean conservation. Her life, a testament to pushing boundaries and defying limitations, finds its ultimate purpose in safeguarding the very element that has been both her playground and her muse. Nyad's connection to the ocean is not merely a love affair; it is a sacred covenant, a deep-seated understanding of the interconnectedness of human life and the delicate balance of the marine ecosystem.

From her early childhood spent swimming in the turquoise waters of Florida, to her record-breaking swims across treacherous currents, the ocean has been a constant presence in her life. As she traversed the vast expanse of water, Nyad observed firsthand the impact of human activities on the marine environment. This firsthand encounter with the fragility of the ocean sparked a fierce passion for conservation, transforming her from an intrepid swimmer into a passionate advocate for the ocean's wellbeing.

While Nyad's achievements in the open water swimming world are undeniable, her greatest legacy may lie in her unwavering commitment to raising awareness about the challenges facing the ocean. Her book, "Find a Way," is not merely a chronicle of her athletic endeavors, but a powerful call to action, urging readers to embrace the responsibility of preserving the planet's most precious resource. Her public speeches, filled with eloquence and fervor, resonate with a powerful message of hope and urgency, urging individuals to act as stewards of the ocean.

Nyad's dedication to ocean conservation finds expression in her active involvement with numerous organizations dedicated to marine conservation. Her role as a spokesperson for the Ocean Conservancy, her participation in campaigns to combat plastic pollution, and her support for research initiatives focused on understanding and protecting marine life are testaments to her commitment to safeguarding the ocean.

Her commitment extends beyond advocating for change. Nyad actively participates in initiatives aimed at implementing sustainable practices. Her support for organizations promoting responsible fishing practices, her engagement in campaigns aimed at reducing ocean pollution, and her tireless efforts in promoting sustainable tourism practices showcase her holistic approach to ocean conservation. Her advocacy goes beyond simply raising awareness; it translates into tangible actions aimed at preserving the ocean's fragile ecosystem.

Nyad's voice is a powerful one, resonating with a global audience captivated by her extraordinary achievements and her passionate advocacy for the ocean. Her journey serves as an inspiration, urging individuals to step beyond the confines of their comfort zones and embrace the responsibility of protecting our planet's most vital resource. Nyad's commitment to ocean conservation stands as a beacon of hope, a testament to the transformative power of one person's unwavering dedication to a cause greater than herself..

Her unwavering commitment transcends the boundaries of athletic achievement, solidifying her position as a true champion for the ocean. Through her voice, her actions, and her tireless efforts, Nyad inspires a global community to embrace the imperative of ocean conservation, reminding us all that the fate of the ocean is inextricably linked to the future of humankind. Her legacy, interwoven with the vast expanse of the ocean she loves, echoes with a powerful message: a call to action, a plea for change, and a profound commitment to preserving the ocean's wonder for generations to come..

## Raising awareness about marine pollution and ocean health

Diana Nyad, the extraordinary athlete who, at 64, conquered the treacherous waters of the Florida Straits, is not just a champion swimmer, but a powerful voice for the ocean's well-being. Her journey from competitive swimmer to environmental advocate is a testament to the profound impact one individual can have on raising awareness about the urgent need to protect our planet's marine ecosystems..

Nyad's accomplishments in the pool are impressive, but her swims across challenging waters are a different story. Her daring feats, like the 110-mile swim from Cuba to Florida, were not simply personal triumphs; they became platforms for highlighting the ocean's fragility. The vastness of the open ocean, a space that inspires awe and wonder, was also a place of environmental peril for Nyad. Her swims were not just about pushing physical boundaries, but also about exposing the invisible threats lurking beneath the waves..

Her experiences in the water, especially during the Cuba-to-Florida swim, brought into sharp focus the alarming realities of marine pollution. She encountered plastic debris, a constant reminder of the human footprint on the ocean. This firsthand encounter with the degradation of our oceans ignited a passionate desire in Nyad to advocate for their preservation..

Nyad's voice resonated with a wider audience because she was not just a spokesperson for environmental protection, but a living example of its necessity. Her grueling swims, with their inherent risks and exposure to pollution, became a powerful metaphor for the challenges facing our oceans. Her triumphs were not just about individual achievement, but also about the courage and resilience needed to safeguard the planet..

In the aftermath of her historic swim, Nyad leveraged her newfound platform to speak out about the threats to ocean health. She became a vocal advocate for reducing plastic pollution, highlighting the devastating consequences of plastic waste on marine life. Her story served as a call to action, inspiring individuals and organizations to take responsibility for their environmental impact and contribute to the preservation of our oceans.

Nyad's work goes beyond raising awareness. She actively supports organizations like the Ocean Conservancy, which focuses on reducing plastic pollution, and the World Wildlife Fund, which works to conserve marine ecosystems. She uses her platform to highlight the interconnectedness of human actions and the health of the planet. .

Nyad's story resonates with the increasing global awareness of environmental issues. Her personal journey, from athletic achievement to environmental advocacy, embodies a crucial shift in our understanding of the human relationship with nature. The ocean is not just a vast expanse, but a delicate ecosystem that requires our active care and protection. Nyad, through her personal experience and her unwavering commitment, inspires us to take action, to be responsible stewards of our planet's oceans. .

Her story serves as a poignant reminder that even the seemingly insurmountable challenges facing our oceans can be addressed through individual action, collective responsibility, and a shared commitment to safeguarding the planet for future generations. By embracing the spirit of Nyad's relentless pursuit of the impossible, we can work towards a future where our oceans are not just resilient, but thrive as vibrant ecosystems.

## Inspiring action through storytelling and activism

Diana Nyad's "Find a Way" is a powerful testament to the transformative potential of storytelling and activism in igniting environmental consciousness and propelling collective action. The book chronicles Nyad's audacious journey to swim from Cuba to Florida, a feat previously deemed impossible. However, it transcends a mere sports narrative; it delves into a profound reflection on human resilience, the indomitable spirit of exploration, and the intricate connection between the individual and the environment.

Nyad's personal narrative becomes a vessel for environmental advocacy, weaving together her athletic prowess, her unwavering determination, and her deep concern for the fragile state of the oceans. The book is not merely a triumphant tale of overcoming physical and mental barriers but a stark reminder of the threats facing our planet's marine ecosystems. She masterfully integrates her personal experience with scientific insights, highlighting the alarming consequences of climate change, plastic pollution, and the depletion of marine life.

Nyad's commitment to environmental advocacy extends beyond mere storytelling. She uses her platform to raise awareness about critical issues, challenging readers to confront their own biases and ignite their own sense of responsibility. By sharing her experiences, she underscores the power of individual action in driving broader societal change. Her journey becomes a metaphor for the collective effort needed to protect our planet.

"Find a Way" doesn't shy away from depicting the complexities of environmental challenges. Nyad acknowledges the daunting scope of these issues, the intricate web of political and economic factors at play, and the need for collaborative solutions. Yet, she emphasizes that despair is not an option. Instead, she urges readers to channel their concerns into meaningful action, whether it's adopting sustainable practices, advocating for policy changes, or simply engaging in open dialogue.

The book's impact extends far beyond the realm of swimming. It inspires a sense of possibility, encouraging individuals to embrace their own personal journeys of exploration and to champion causes they believe in. Nyad's story serves as a call to action, urging readers to step out of their comfort zones, to confront their fears, and to contribute to a healthier and more sustainable future.

"Find a Way" is not simply a story about a remarkable feat of athleticism. It's a poignant testament to the transformative power of storytelling and activism in igniting environmental consciousness and propelling collective action. By weaving together her personal experience with scientific insights and a profound sense of purpose, Nyad empowers *readers to embrace a deeper connection to the planet and to champion a more sustainable future. The book transcends the boundaries of individual achievement, becoming a call to action for a global community committed to environmental stewardship.*

Made in the USA
Monee, IL
15 December 2025

38421780R00059